Digital Analytics

The Path from Clicks to Conversions

Dr. Kyle Allison

Printed in the United States of America

ISBN 979-8-9894097-0-9

Dedication

This book is dedicated to many mentors, colleagues and peers in my professional and academic career who has influenced my passion in the field of digital business and analytics. Also, this book is dedicated to my wife, Melissa, for her continuous love, support, and partnership in this life.

Preface

Today's modern digital analyst is inundated with more big data, complex business scenarios, and challenges than ever before. The 2020's has elevated the dialogue in businesses on the importance of being data-driven in decision making and strategy planning. For that reason, while digital analytics is not a brand-new field, the way in which we adopt such practices and build maturity in our organizations as a standard way of conducting digital strategy and e-commerce business planning is still on the horizon of advancement and change.

The other dynamic is that digital analytics has broadened in its usage from digital marketing campaign analysis, website experience analysis, customer relationship analytics, sales analytics and more. There is no one-size-fits-all digital analytics approach to all various dynamics of digital business. That is the part of maturity that is needed for organizations to embrace. The focus of one digital analytics method or approach varies based on what exactly is being sought for in strategy, solutions, or answers. Therefore, there is more art and science in this analytics discipline than many others.

The core focus of this book is to focus moreover on the web funnel of analytics. There is plenty of metrics and methods to analyze performance of outbound digital marketing that drives traffic to websites, which is where many companies have adopted and have varying degrees of how useful and mature, they are at using the analytics to strengthen those outbound marketing efforts. To understand outbound marketing, consider digital advertising such as social media, email marketing, blogs, paid ads on Google and more.

But there is a common problem: many companies tend to focus too much on the early stages of their marketing efforts, like online ads and getting people interested to visit a website. They often overlook what happens after that, as people move through the entire journey of becoming customers on a website experience. This book aims at diving in deeper into the web funnel and guiding the elements of metrics, analysis, and overall approach to understand how to optimize digital website experiences to drive website visitors to conversion and building loyalty and destination equity.

The goal of this book is straightforward: to provide a complete guide that not only recognizes the importance of analyzing digital ads and the start of the customer journey but also looks deeper into what happens afterward—the entire "web funnel." The goal is to guide businesses, marketers, and analysts with the knowledge and tools they need to understand what is happening at every step of the customer journey. By doing this, the hope is to connect the dots between marketing and the overall digital user experience. Focusing on what to analyze and assess on the path of web users from clicks to conversions.

Table of Contents

Chapter One: Digital Analytics Today

1.1 Introduction

As technology continues to evolve, so does the corporate environment. In fact, technological advancements have greatly impacted how companies operate and provide goods and services within their respective markets. The prevalence of the internet and the emergence of new software have both increased the level of competition across the business landscape and bolstered our ability to capture a vast amount of data and information. This increase in available information can help organizations set their strategic visions. It has also created the need to ensure that the data is properly and responsibly gathered and managed.

Companies must guarantee that the data are valid, useful, and generally able to be consolidated and analyzed. The need to analyze the various elements of business (e.g., customer behavior, sales, operational planning, forecasting, or digital marketing) has become competitive, and this analysis must be used to meet the demands of customers. Digital analytics is a concept born out of an organization's need to take these data points and animate them. In doing so, the organization gains insights, perspectives, and direct evidence of dynamics within the business that support effective strategic decision-making.

Digital analytics has come with a great need to support strategic proposals planning, and execution, and also has become a core element in business today. This unit will begin with a holistic view of what digital analytics is, how it is built, what it means to have successful analytics, and, most importantly, how to leverage digital analytics to support strategy in today's corporate environment. In this unit, we start with basic definitions, the scope of goals in digital analytics, and an overview of data and information sources, followed with a conclusion regarding the corresponding legal framework within this field.

Defining Digital Analytics

At its core, **digital analytics** is defined as the process of gathering, storing, measuring, and analyzing information and data from digital sources (e.g., websites, social media, or mobile applications). The process provides organizations with the ability to understand the behavior of the customers and users of their digital channels and platforms. Additionally, it generates new insights that can help support or shape a new strategic vision and eventual plans for the organization.

Depending on the needs for a particular analysis, the insights from the data could be qualitative, quantitative, or both. **Qualitative** measurements focus on subjective viewpoints or traits of user behavior within a digital channel based on the assessment of quality. For example, one could measure how satisfied any given customer is with their experience. The level of satisfaction here would be a qualitative measurement based on the opinion and subjectivity of the user. **Quantitative** measurements, conversely, focus on fixed, descriptive numeric values based on factual and transactional data. For example, one could look at the number of online visitors to a website. This demonstrates a quantity of behavior and factual account of a digital activity.

Digital analytics serves to focus both on marketing engagement and online website behavior. It can provide evidentiary support and information to marketers, website designers, sales teams, and other key business stakeholders, aiding them in making effective, data-driven decisions. Today, there is a prime opportunity to continue guiding organizational culture change through the adoption of digital analytics as a key component of the strategic planning process.

Data analytics emerged at the onset of digital marketing. Once internet technology was made available and extensible to the public, search engines and social media platforms became distinct online marketing fields that students and professionals could research and master. With the growth of these channels, companies quickly needed to learn how to adapt if they were to become players in the digital market. The internet, with its rapid pace, allows for an open market. In other words, business can simply go online and take part in this globally connected environment with both customers and other businesses alike. This means, however, that an organization must ensure that both its corporate strategies and the business it conducts are optimal.

Evolution of Digital Analytics

Since the early 2000s, as mainstream companies found their way online (both to market and eventually start selling their products online), the desire to learn about customer behavior increased. In the decades prior, companies relied on analytics based on passive or descriptive information, i.e., transactional information (e.g., sales, returns, satisfaction scores from mail-in surveys, or focus groups). These methods are considered traditional, chiefly serving business conducted outside of the digital channels.

The growth of the internet and digital business led to an increased curiosity concerning what was really happening behind the screen of the user. Given that there was no direct, clear insight regarding where, why, or how customers made decisions when interacting with digital channels and marketing content, organizations were left with only their imaginations.

Sales information alone did not paint the complete picture that website designers, marketers, and those in charge of the digital experience required in order to ensure that the online content was engaging and serving its intended purpose, i.e., driving traffic to the intended websites and social channels. It was at this point companies started recognizing this gap and understanding the need for proper data collection of this digital user activity, particularly to support their strategic initiatives and business plans.

Digital analytics was born from these core needs. Nevertheless, for many companies of the early 2000s, the question remained: how can we sculpt a digital analytics infrastructure to manage all of these data?

Over time, as the World Wide Web continued to offer many industries and companies a digital channel for selling their products and services, marketing to and communicating with their customers, and providing a differentiated competitive experience beyond physical footprint, it became clearer what type of customer data could be obtained. With this new knowledge came shifts in the organizational culture at certain companies, which were starting to adopt the methods and mindset needed to construct, implement, and leverage a digital analytics system as part of their strategic planning. Even today, we continue to learn, and many companies and industries are still trying to pave their own path with the use of digital analytics.

1.2 Goals of Digital Analytics

Digital analytics offers a wide variety of uses concerning the ways a company can leverage its benefits. At the core of this concept, the one ultimate goal is to understand customers and their behavior. With this comes the secondary goal of better supporting any strategic initiatives designed to influence said behavior, e.g., to steer a customer into doing something different. Prior to the emergence of the digital environment, understanding competitive behavior was done using traditional marketing research methods. Additionally, companies would use quantitative insights, such as sales or revenue, to help determine the strength of a product, marketing campaign, or shopping experience. While these data insights held some relevant validity, they did not encompass all of the users' decision points and their overall behavioral patterns. Digital analytics allows us to narrow the scope and take a more initiative-taking viewpoint on customer behavior.

Business author Judah Phillips (2016) outlines the "Analytics Value Chain" with the following six steps:

1. **Understand what to analyze.** This step requires an analysis of business requirements and data structure. Identifying the appropriate data elements provides the foundation for the development of the analytics process.
2. **Collect and verify the data.** In this step, the ability to collect the appropriate data is assessed and the integrity of the information verified. Data governance and an oversight on the quality of the data are crucial here.
3. **Report and verify.** This step sees the creation, verification, and public release of dashboards, reports, and other reference materials.
4. **Analyze, communicate, and socialize.** This step provides the actions that must be taken based on the data insights. It draws in key stakeholders and the appropriate business audience to ensure that the information is appropriately shared and delivered in a timely fashion and actions are administered. Also, narratives and stories are constructed and presented for discussion.
5. **Optimize and predict.** In this step, one can work with a predictive analytics model that lets the data insights derive a future viewpoint on the strategies implemented.
6. **Demonstrate economic value.** At this last step, one can ensure the most suitable financial metrics are considered and measured, i.e., those which evaluate the overall performance of and impact on an analytics assessment. For digital analytics, the primary goal is to understand user or consumer behavior as it relates to:

    - website experiences
    - shopping behavior
    - social media engagement
    - digital marketing engagement (e.g., email blasts and banner advertisements)
    - search engine optimization
    - other digital channels and vehicle strategy optimization

Marketing Strategy and Engagement

Digital analytics should support digital marketing strategy, with the goal being to explain user engagement. Marketing engagement is a practice where we attempt to gain a customer's attention and reaction based on advertising campaigns and user experiences. It should also serve to validate the plans for marketing campaigns, particularly concerning the imagery, content, messaging, and value proposition from which a design team can learn in order to render their creative elements more impactful. Overall, digital analytics has the ability to help the digital marketer know what content resonates, how often to market, and in what digital channel to market. In order to understand a customer's entire interaction and journey with digital marketing, digital analytics provides a holistic viewport of this individual.

Another goal within the realm of using digital analytics to support marketing strategy is to focus on customer segmentation and targeted marketing techniques. In targeted marketing, a group is defined according to certain criteria, with those in that group considered most likely to purchase a given product. Then, those products are marketed to that group. Companies create marketing plans and unique goods for these preferred consumer segments once the main groups have been established. Through the use of digital analytics, marketers can develop their focus around which advertisements and experiences are best suited to which audiences, i.e., offer tailored experiences.

It is important to understand the audience's behaviors and characteristics, e.g., their needs, consumption patterns, and locations. This awareness helps facilitate the effective delivery of an advertising campaign. Targeted marketing offers major benefits, specifically the ability to disseminate messages to a specific audience that will most likely respond. The US Data Corporation (n.d.) offers an example: "If a florist wants to reach couples to promote for Valentine's Day, they can use a mailing list targeted towards married couples living within a five-mile radius of the florist" (para. 3). By targeting the correct audience, a company can increase its campaign's performance, thereby improving sales and return on investment (ROI). Finding the right balance between workable content and the appropriate methods for communicating said content to the right customer (and at the right time) falls within the scope of marketing engagement. Marketing analytics, in its essence, will primarily focus on campaigns and optimizing marketing technology (US Data Corporation, n.d.).

Web Analytics and Web Behavior

In this aspect of digital analytics, we are concerned with the overall user and visitor experience on a website. Questions that are generally explored in this type of web analysis include:

- Where are visitors going?
- Where on the website are they living?
- What is causing user irritants in navigation and on-site search?
- What web layout and design elements are attracting or losing visitors?
- Are the website visitors converting?
- What is the overall path and funnel we are looking to optimize?

Figure 1.1 Digital Funnel

Understanding the digital funnel, which reflects the layers of a website visitor's digital journey, is key to web analytics. The funnel starts with the awareness layer, which reflects what attracted a user to visit a website. Then, as a website visitor searches, browses, or navigates a website, they move to the interest level, which mirrors some level of curiosity in the visitor's behavior. Then, there is an evaluation and consideration process concerning what that website visitor wants to do, reflected in any actions actually taken on the website. This action, for example, could be completing a purchase, registering for a service, or filling out an application. At this point, the conversion metric becomes important. Throughout the visitor's entire digital journey, from awareness to action, various methods exist for analyzing specific digital strategy goals (Wilkes, n.d.).

Overall, the primary goal of digital analytics is to understand any given user's digital journey, from the outbound digital marketing element to their path to a website, and ultimately, at the point of interaction with the website. Optimizing and enhancing those digital experiences derive from a data-driven decision-making process that makes use of mature digital analytics methods and insights.

1.3 Data and Information Sources

Let us take a closer look at what types of data are and how they can be categorized and processed for digital analytics use. Furthermore, it is important to understand what role the internet plays. Finally, we will look at the many methods that we can use to collect data. Now, we ask ourselves where data can be found and how they can help us discover more.

Data: Structure versus Unstructured

To start the process of developing a digital analytics platform, team, and overall process for an organization, we must start with an understanding of two distinct types of data: structured and unstructured.

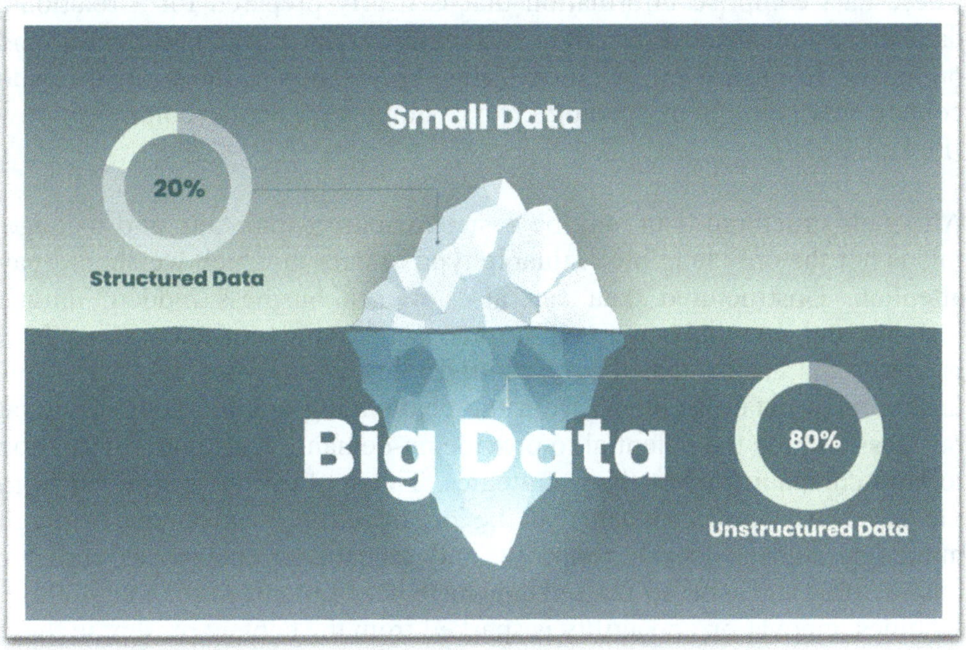

Figure 1.2 Structured vs Unstructured Data

The most common type of data before the emergence of digital business was structured data. This type of data is organized with finite values and attributes. Financial data, including revenue, costs, accounts, and other set values, provide perfect examples. Structured data are generally easier to review and synthesize when reviewing analytics and reports. They are also more efficiently managed and stored, leading to the development of the analytics from a relational database or spreadsheet.

Structured data also tend to be easier to understand and interpret by their very nature. Unstructured data, by comparison, are less organized and tend not to exist in a database of rows and columns. The information is not as complete and poses a challenge to the company attempting to operate their analytics, namely that they may not easily adapt to the analytical database and may not be understood by the tool in use by said company. Therefore, special technology tools are built to read and modify the information to ensure it is tangible and able to be validated for analytics use (Pickell, 2021).

With this in mind, there are three sub-types of data: data that are convenient for data scientists (and perhaps market analysts) to organize and from which to derive value, data that are not convenient for this, and data that are both. The main difference between structured data and unstructured data lies in their inherent degrees of usefulness and ability to be optimized, i.e., to be structural in nature, thus meeting an organization's analytical needs. That final data type, semi-structured data, is a combination of both of these. These data comprise information that is nearly prepared for a relational database or spreadsheet, i.e., they still require some areas to be cleaned and organized to ensure proper processing. For example, those areas could contain misspellings or spacing errors within a particular column or row (Pickell, 2018).

Although structured data may be easier to source, maintain, and manage, this is not the only tangible, valuable type of data to which we should pay attention. Unstructured data can also offer a business hidden, unique insights, and potential benefits if the analyst takes the time to organize them properly and ensure that they are fitted into the analytics database. This unstructured data also stems from the challenging environment of digital business and has the potential to provide on-demand, real-time information to help companies pivot their strategies. The applications generated from the newly standardized data can be organized and exchanged through numerous industry-based, nonprofit, and educational enterprises until the unstructured and semi-structured data have been organized for analytic use. At times, innovation and agility is sparked from the content present in these unstructured data (Pickell, 2018).

The World Wide Web

The ability to understand digital analytics also stems from a need to understand how the internet and the World Wide Web (or, simply, "the Web") fundamentally operate and how that affects the ways in which structured or unstructured data are captured. Comprising various technologies, the internet is a global network of interconnected devices, such as computers, smartphones, switches, routers, satellites, and cables. It also acts as a kind of phone book or digital directory, capable of converting an almost infinite number of names into numbers (and vice versa). The World Wide Web is a collection of protocols and services that enable these devices to communicate with one another, and it serves as the foundation for the study of digital analytics (Sponder & Khan, 2018). It is composed of interconnected hypertext documents (e.g., websites) that can be viewed via internet browsers (e.g., Google Chrome or Firefox) in its most basic form (Google, n.d.; Mozilla, n.d.-a.).

A proper device mechanism for storing, managing, and building an organization's analytics infrastructure is necessary at the interaction points between the data capturing digital devices and channels present on the World Wide Web. The transmission of these data is needed to gather and compile the elements relevant to user behavior and engagement insights.

Data Integrity and Data Quality

According to Paquette (2020), the data collected can be affected by a lack of completeness concerning their content. He poses several questions, asking what the data represent, why they were collected, and what their purpose may be: "Typically, the missing information [...] is stored in the brains of domain experts, i.e., specific humans. And those humans are rarely in the same place as the data sources they own or once owned" (para. 4). In the end, the data being transmitted also needs validation. In other words, a level of data integrity is imperative.

Proper understanding of the need to ensure a proper information process (i.e., that the information is scoped out, appropriated, and ultimately collected from trusted sources) is critical to the success of digital analytics. While a company may be able to employ techniques to manage both the structured and unstructured data, it must also understand the existing conditions and variables when understanding the digital sources and where the data originate: Are the data coming from a pure quantitative perspective for application? Or, conversely, are we working with a bias subjective set of data requiring awareness and attribution (when used in a digital analytics context)? Analysts must ask themselves if they can trust the data and if they understand their origins well enough to be able to provide the insights they wish to present.

Once it can be verified that the data originates from a trust source, then comes the need to ensure their quality. To be useful in decision-making, data must be complete, special, accurate, timely, and dependable. While integrity focuses on the data's trustworthiness, data quality entails their validation and determines whether they will derive at the viewpoints and insights needed to form effective strategic decisions.

Information Sources and Data Collection

Data gathering and processing is the method of acquiring, extracting, and storing substantial amounts of data in structured or unstructured formats (e.g., text, images, video, audio, or XML files) that will be used later during analysis (SAS Institute, n.d.). Information collection is the first step in the big data research process before beginning to evaluate the trends or useful knowledge therein. The data to be analyzed must be gathered from a variety of reliable sources, and it is imperative that these data are rich in detail. The information gathered is known as intelligence, and the data collected (which are not usable in their current state) are called raw data. After cleaning the impure data and using it for further study, the information obtained is then known as knowledge.

The majority of the data collected can fit into one of two types: qualitative and quantitative. Qualitative data are a compilation of non-numerical data (e.g., words and sentences) that focus on the group's attitudes and actions; quantitative data, by comparison, are measured numerically (Niraula, 2019). When the data are still in their rawest state, i.e., derived directly from official documents, we call these data "primary." If the data collected fails to satisfy the needs and expectations of the target group involved in the study, this entire process can become quite burdensome. In order to ensure that the data are suitable for their intended purpose, we can employ various methods at this stage, including specific interview, survey, observation, experimental, and scientific statistical methods (Pickell, 2021).

Data that has already been compiled and reused for a valid purpose is considered secondary data. This kind of information is previously derived from either internal or external primary sources. Internal sources consist of several types of data (e.g., market records, revenue records, transactions, customer data, and accounting information) and are readily accessible within the enterprise. They are less expensive and take less time to procure. By comparison, external sources (e.g., agency reports, press publications, and business research sites) have a varying degree of accessibility and options. External source evidence is information that cannot be contained within an entity and must be accessed from third-party sources. Since this involves working with a large volume of data, the associated costs are higher, and more time is required for processing.

Data Sources

For digital analytics, information sources come in varied forms and provide a combined effort to aid in the understanding of a consumer's digital journey. We will now take a look at some of the several types of digital data sources as outlined by Angel (2015).

Online and in-store data

In the retail space, data derived from both digital and in-store channels can provide valuable insights into overall consumer behavior and experiences once they are compared with each other. This also offers the perspective from a hybrid or omni-channel approach. Sales data fit together with virtually every data form on various methods from surveys, web browsing, and other sources, resulting in new experiences and personalization possibilities. The prospects for customized advertising are worthy of analysis for targeted marketing efforts. For example, we may use details of in-store purchases to draft and issue a customized newsletter showcasing items from the online store (or vice versa).

Web browsing data

The company's audience should be able to make buying decisions as a result of its content marketing efforts. To show the relation between the decision-making and the marketing efforts (and explain the budget), the company needs to link the web browsing data to sales data. A true understanding of how the audience engages with the marketing content is imperative, as it allows the company to propose and make its next moves and deals (e.g., which options they should deliver and how to implement them).

Survey data

Companies often conduct consumer surveys in-store, over the phone, or online. They can keep track of their net promoter score (NPS), product and service satisfaction, and employee helpfulness. But where does this information end up? The company should maintain a database (for each person) that records which surveys they have taken and what their answers are. When new survey data are combined with data from this database, the company benefits from a fuller image that aids in problem identification.

Customer service data

This type of data provides the analyst with a window into how service influences consumer behavior. By looking at call volumes, tallying the types of issues raised, and understanding overall service satisfaction, the analyst can provide insights on how a company could increase its customer satisfaction or service value proposition.

Advertising platform

When using any type of marketing technology or CRM software platform, the rich data that can be obtained from customers interacting with marketing content and campaigns are invaluable. These data help identify which parts of the marketing content grabs the customer's attention and, thus, what works and what does not. This can help build marketing strategy and reveal further insights for other areas of the business (e.g., product development, supply and demand needs, and operational service elements).

Loyalty data

What motivates the consumers to participate in a company's loyalty program? How can a company use these insights to draw in more customers? The solution may lie in exclusive offers, presents, or invitations to events for preferred customers. Conversely, perhaps, it could come in the form of social media engagement with the brand or offers of early access to highly awaited launches. Loyalty services can amass data that are rather helpful for further targeting the right audience.

Legacy data

Looking back at older evidence can be worthwhile, as this information helps a company understand its customers' experiences and how they may change over time. Any companies currently storing data that remain unlinked to their platform would be best served implementing them as soon as possible.

Cloud Data Sources

Software as a Service (SaaS) providers, such as cloud-based data stores Amazon Web Services or Rackspace, have been offering externally hosted resources for storage and tooling data for many years (Amazon Web Services, n.d.; Rackspace, n.d.). In certain instances, rather than deploying the enterprise data warehouse (EDW) in an on-premises database, the cloud provider may only have infrastructure for the client to install and access purchased applications. A vendor-hosted cloud service allows for the sending of data to the vendor through an application programming interface (API), a batch process such as the Simple File Transfer Protocol (SFTP), or the implementation of a proprietary data loader.

This loader sits on company servers, automatically searches the data, and then transfers said data to the cloud vendor in near real time. An analyst needs to understand how to navigate cloud-based data (and how to link their tools to them). A company would want to collaborate with its respective internet technology (IT) and data governance departments to ensure that the data going to the cloud adheres to the established data definitions and analytical requirements.

Cloud environments may be single or multitenant, i.e., private, and public. Servers in a distributed cloud are used by several different clients simultaneously, meaning that their personal data are often physically stored alongside the data of another client. For this reason, multitenant clouds are referred to as public clouds. By comparison, in a private cloud, the servers hold only the data of one particular client, and only this client has access to the servers.

Other Data Sources

Overall, the types of data and information sources vary, and it is up to each individual organization to determine which data it needs and find the appropriate credible sources. In doing so, the necessary data feed can be generated, ensuring that the only information gathered will impact the organization's digital strategies. Aside from those previously mentioned, there are other relevant data sources that track user behavior.

Web server logs, for example, offer an unfiltered view of a website's traffic. They come in the form of plain text files on the web server. Any time a plugin or user agent (such as a web crawler or search engine) demands a resource from the server—whether that be a page, photo, JavaScript file, or anything else—the server adds a line to the log (Lurie, 2019).

Cookies, another source of data, are text files containing small bits of information (e.g., a username or password). These are used to mark a device when it connects to the internet. HTTP cookies are used to recognize and enhance the web surfing experience by allowing the end user to identify other browsers (Mozilla, n.d.-b). We also have device IDs, a series of numbers and letters that uniquely identifies each smartphone or tablet in use across the globe. This ID, saved on the device, can be used by any software that has been downloaded, installed, and enabled on it (Adjust, n.d.). All of these additional data sources help widen the scope for the digital analyst and marketer. With this information, it is easier to identify how customers behave and what their interests are, aided in particular by the knowledge regarding how they access certain websites and content.

Key Points:

1. Technological advancements, particularly the internet and new software, have significantly influenced corporate operations and competition.
2. Digital analytics is vital for understanding customer behavior and informing strategic decision-making.
3. It encompasses both qualitative (subjective user opinions) and quantitative (numerical data) aspects of customer interactions.
4. The evolution of digital analytics has shifted from traditional methods to a more comprehensive understanding of online customer behavior.
5. Digital analytics supports various business aspects, including marketing strategy, web behavior analysis, and targeted advertising.
6. It is crucial to distinguish between structured, unstructured, and semi-structured data for effective digital analytics.
7. Understanding the role of the World Wide Web and maintaining data integrity and quality are essential for reliable analytics.
8. Different data sources, including online surveys, customer service, loyalty programs, and cloud sources, provide valuable insights.
9. Legacy data can offer historical perspectives, aiding in understanding changes in consumer behavior over time.
10. Understanding and effectively leveraging digital analytics is an ongoing process that continues to evolve with technology and market trends.

Discussion Questions:

1. How has the shift from traditional to digital analytics changed the way companies understand and interact with their customers?
2. In what ways can companies ensure the validity and reliability of the data they collect for digital analytics?
3. How does the balance between qualitative and quantitative data affect the insights gained from digital analytics?
4. What challenges do companies face when integrating several types of data (structured, unstructured, semi-structured) into their analytics platforms?
5. How can businesses effectively use digital analytics to predict future customer behaviors and market trends?

Chapter Two:

Web Data Collection Methods

2.1 Introduction

The digital world is an ever-expanding universe of data. Every click, every search, every social interaction on the web generates data points that, when collected and analyzed, can offer invaluable insights into human behavior, market trends, and societal shifts.

Comprehensive Web Data Sources

1. **Websites and E-commerce Platforms:** These sources provide insights into user engagement, purchasing patterns, and product preferences. By analyzing this data, businesses can optimize their websites, tailor their marketing strategies, and enhance customer experiences.
2. **Social Media Analytics:** Platforms such as Facebook, Twitter, LinkedIn, and Instagram provide a rich source of data regarding user opinions, trends, demographic information, and engagement metrics. Social media analytics helps in understanding brand perception, tracking campaign performance, and gauging public opinion on diverse topics.
3. **APIs and Web Services:** APIs from services like Google Maps, weather information, or stock market data provide structured, reliable data for various applications. They enable businesses to integrate external data sources seamlessly into their systems.
4. **Public and Government Datasets:** These datasets are often underutilized but contain valuable information on a wide range of topics, from public health to economic indicators. Analyzing these datasets can provide insights into broader trends and patterns affecting various sectors.

Advanced Data Collection Methods

1. **Sophisticated Web Scraping:** Advanced web scraping involves not just extracting data but also automating the process using bots and crawlers. These tools can navigate through web pages, identify relevant information, and extract it in a structured format for further analysis.

2. **Interactive APIs:** Beyond simple data retrieval, interactive APIs allow for real-time data exchange between different web services, enabling dynamic data collection and immediate insights.
3. **Online Surveys and Polls:** Digital surveys and polls can be strategically designed to gather specific information directly from the target audience. Advanced tools enable the creation of interactive, engaging surveys that can improve response rates and data quality.
4. **Behavioral Data Tracking:** This involves tracking user actions like clicks, mouse movements, and scrolling patterns on websites. Tools like session replays and heatmap analysis provide insights into user behavior and website usability.

Web Data Collection Methods

Web scraping and web crawling are two fundamental methods used for collecting data from the internet, each with distinct purposes, processes, and applications in the field of web analytics.

Web Scraping

Definition: Web scraping is a technique employed to extract specific information or data elements from web pages. It is commonly used to gather structured data, such as product prices, customer reviews, news articles, and more.

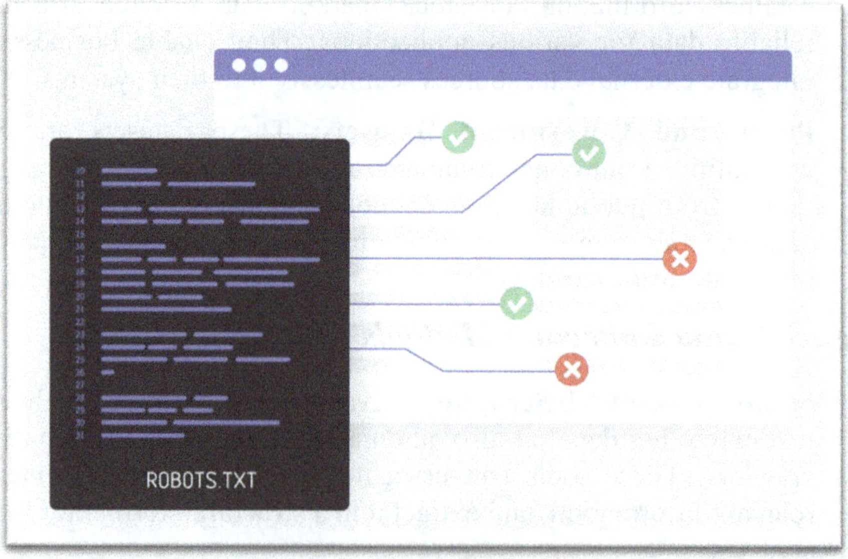

Figure 2.1 Web Scraping

How It Works:

1. **Sending HTTP Request**: A web scraping tool or script initiates an HTTP request to a target website's server to retrieve the HTML content of a specific webpage.
2. **Parsing HTML**: The retrieved HTML content is parsed to identify and locate the relevant data elements, such as tables, paragraphs, or headings.
3. **Data Extraction**: Using selectors or patterns, the scraper extracts the desired data elements from the HTML source code, often by locating elements based on their HTML tags, attributes, or using advanced techniques like XPath or CSS selectors.
4. **Data Transformation**: Extracted data may undergo additional processing or cleaning to ensure it is in a usable format, which is crucial for maintaining data quality.
5. **Data Storage**: The scraped data is typically stored in a structured format, such as a database, spreadsheet, or JSON file, for further analysis using web analytics tools.

Use Cases: Web scraping has a wide range of applications, including:

- Price monitoring for e-commerce.
- Content aggregation for news websites.
- Gathering user reviews and ratings.
- Market research and competitive analysis.
- Lead generation and contact information retrieval.

Web Crawling

Definition: Web crawling, also known as web indexing, is the process of systematically navigating and indexing the entire internet or a specific portion of it. It is primarily used by search engines to discover and catalog web pages, making them searchable for users.

How It Works:

1. **Starting Point**: A web crawler begins with a list of seed URLs or a known starting point. It explores each URL, parsing its HTML content.

2. **Discovering Links**: While parsing a webpage, the crawler identifies hyperlinks to other pages. These links are then added to a queue for further exploration.
3. **Queue Management**: The crawler systematically processes the links in its queue, visiting each page, parsing its content, and repeating the process of discovering new links.
4. **Indexing**: Information about each visited webpage is collected and indexed in a database. This index is used by search engines to provide search results to users.
5. **Respect Robots.txt**: Crawler bots typically adhere to the rules specified in a website's **robots.txt** file, which can restrict or guide the crawling process.

Web crawling is primarily used for:

- Search engine indexing and retrieval.
- Building website directories and sitemaps.
- Monitoring website health and detecting broken links.
- Analyzing website structure and hierarchy.

The primary differences between web scraping and web crawling lie in their objectives, scope, and the way they interact with websites.

Web scraping is highly focused and designed for extracting specific, structured data from individual web pages. It targets elements within a webpage, such as product prices, article headlines, or contact information, and extracts them for analysis. Web scraping is typically initiated by users or automated scripts with predefined criteria, making it a more controlled and narrow approach. It is particularly useful when you need to collect data from a limited number of websites and when the data you seek is consistent in its structure.

On the other hand, web crawling is a broad and continuous process aimed at indexing a vast number of web pages across the internet. Search engines like Google use web crawling to discover, index, and make web content searchable for users. Unlike web scraping, web crawling explores a wide range of websites, following hyperlinks to navigate the web's interconnected structure. It operates autonomously, systematically traversing the web and collecting information about websites and their relationships. Web crawling is indispensable for creating comprehensive search engine databases and building the foundation for effective web searches.

In summary, web scraping is a targeted, data-extraction technique for specific web pages, while web crawling is a comprehensive process designed to index and catalog the entire web. The choice between these methods depends on the objectives of data collection and the scale of web analysis required for a given project or application.

2.2 Implementing Tracking Codes

Tracking codes are the backbone of data collection on websites. They provide insights into user behavior, traffic sources, and on-site interactions. In this comprehensive exploration, we delve into the world of tracking technologies, covering advanced implementations, best practices, challenges, and considerations.

Advanced Tracking Code Implementations

1. **Google Analytics Enhanced Ecommerce:** This tool tracks user interactions with products on e-commerce sites, including product impressions, clicks, and checkout behavior. It provides deeper insights into shopping behavior and helps in optimizing the sales funnel.
2. **Conversion Tracking Pixels:** Used extensively in online advertising, these pixels track user actions after they interact with an ad, providing insights into the effectiveness of ad campaigns.
3. **Custom Event Tracking:** Advanced implementations involve setting up custom events to track specific interactions on a website. This can include form submissions, video plays, or interactions with a particular feature.

Best Practices in Tracking Code Implementation

1. **Privacy-First Approach:** With increasing concerns around user privacy, it is essential to implement tracking codes in a way that respects user consent and complies with privacy laws.
2. **Cross-Device Tracking:** Implement tracking codes that can track user behavior across different devices, providing a unified view of the customer journey.
3. **Data Layer Integration:** Using a data layer can help in managing and organizing the data collected from various sources. It acts as a central repository, simplifying data handling and ensuring accuracy.

4. **Performance Optimization:** Efficient tracking code implementation is crucial for website performance. Minimizing the impact on page load times and resource consumption is essential to provide a smooth user experience.
5. **A/B Testing Integration:** Incorporating tracking codes with A/B testing tools allows you to measure the impact of distinctive design or content variations on user behavior, enabling data-driven decisions for website optimization.
6. **User Segmentation:** Utilize tracking codes to segment your audience based on their behavior, demographics, or other criteria. This enables personalized marketing strategies and content recommendations.
7. **Goal Tracking and Conversion Funnel Analysis:** Set up tracking codes to monitor specific goals on your website, such as sign-ups or purchases, and analyze the conversion funnel to identify bottlenecks and opportunities for improvement.
8. **Real-time Reporting:** Implement tracking codes that provide real-time data reporting, allowing you to react swiftly to emerging trends and make timely adjustments to your marketing and user experience strategies.
9. **Third-party Integration:** Ensure compatibility with third-party platforms and tools, such as CRM systems or email marketing software, to streamline data sharing and enhance the overall customer experience.

Advanced Tracking Code Challenges and Considerations

While advanced tracking code implementations offer valuable insights, they also present challenges:

1. **Data Accuracy:** To maintain data accuracy, regular auditing and validation of tracking codes are necessary. Changes to the website structure or third-party integrations can impact data quality.
2. **Privacy Compliance:** Stay up to date with evolving privacy regulations, such as GDPR and CCPA, to ensure your tracking codes adhere to legal requirements and respect user rights.
3. **Resource Allocation:** Implementing and maintaining advanced tracking codes requires resources, both in terms of personnel and technology. Consider the costs and benefits carefully.

4. **User Experience:** Balancing data collection with a seamless user experience is essential. Too many tracking codes or intrusive data requests can negatively impact website usability.
5. **Data Security:** Protect the data collected through tracking codes with robust security measures to prevent breaches or unauthorized access.
6. **Continuous Improvement:** Keep up with industry trends and evolving technologies to ensure your tracking code implementation remains effective and up to date.

Conclusion

Deep diving into tracking technologies reveals a world of possibilities for businesses seeking to understand and optimize user behavior on their websites. Advanced tracking code implementations offer rich insights, but they come with responsibilities and challenges. By adopting best practices in implementation, maintaining data accuracy, and staying compliant with privacy regulations, businesses can harness the power of tracking codes to drive informed decision-making and improve user experiences. Balancing data collection with user privacy and website performance is the key to successfully navigating this dynamic landscape of tracking technologies.

2.3 Privacy and Ethics in Data Collection

Privacy and Ethics in Data Collection

In today's digital landscape, where data breaches and privacy concerns are on the rise, ethical data collection practices are not just a legal obligation but also a vital element of establishing and maintaining consumer trust. This section explores the complex web of data privacy, international privacy laws and standards, and strategies for deepening ethical practices in data collection.

International Privacy Laws and Standards

1. **GDPR (General Data Protection Regulation):** GDPR, which applies to companies operating in the European Union, has set a global benchmark for data protection. It places significant emphasis on transparency, obtaining user consent, and upholding the right to privacy. GDPR has encouraged organizations worldwide to rethink their data collection practices.
2. **CCPA (California Consumer Privacy Act):** CCPA, akin to GDPR, grants California residents more control over their personal

information. It mandates the disclosure of what data is being collected and the purposes for which it is used. CCPA has inspired similar privacy regulations in other U.S. states.

3. **PIPEDA (Personal Information Protection and Electronic Documents Act):** In Canada, PIPEDA establishes standards for private sector organizations concerning the collection, use, and disclosure of personal information in commercial activities. It underscores the importance of informed consent and data protection.

Data privacy laws have a significant impact on web analytics by imposing strict regulations on the collection, storage, and use of user data. These laws, such as the General Data Protection Regulation (GDPR) in Europe and the California Consumer Privacy Act (CCPA) in the United States, aim to protect individuals' privacy rights in the digital age.

One key aspect of these regulations is the requirement for businesses to obtain explicit consent from users before collecting and processing their personal data. Websites must provide clear and easily accessible privacy notices that explain what data is being collected and for what purposes, including tracking user behavior and gathering information like IP addresses, device identifiers, and browsing history.

Additionally, data privacy laws mandate that websites offer users the option to opt out of data collection and tracking. This poses a challenge for web analytics, potentially reducing the amount of data available for analysis. However, respecting users' choices and ensuring compliance with opt-out mechanisms is crucial.

Businesses must also adhere to stringent security measures to safeguard user data from breaches, given the sensitive nature of the information involved in web analytics. Moreover, these laws dictate data retention and deletion requirements, impacting the historical data accessible for analysis in web analytics tools.

Lastly, data subjects have the right to access, correct, delete, or port their personal data under privacy laws. Consequently, businesses utilizing web analytics tools must establish procedures to promptly and accurately respond to such requests, a task that can be complex when dealing with substantial datasets.

In summary, data privacy laws significantly influence web analytics by necessitating user consent, offering opt-out choices, enforcing data security, influencing data retention policies, and granting users control over their data. Compliance with these regulations is essential for businesses to conduct effective web analytics while respecting user privacy.

Deepening Ethical Practices in Data Collection

1. **Consent Management Platforms:** To ensure ethical data collection, organizations often implement consent management platforms. These platforms facilitate the clear and unambiguous acquisition of user consent, respecting user preferences and adhering to legal requirements. They play a vital role in building trust with users.
2. **Data Minimization:** Ethical data collection practices involve gathering only the data that is necessary for the intended purpose. Data minimization reduces the risk of data misuse, ensures that users' privacy is respected, and minimizes the data storage burden.
3. **Anonymization and Pseudonymization:** To safeguard user privacy and security, organizations often employ techniques like anonymization and pseudonymization. These methods transform personal data in a way that prevents direct identification, thus enhancing data protection.
4. **Regular Audits and Compliance Checks:** Ethical data collectors conduct periodic audits of their data collection practices. These audits help identify and rectify any potential ethical or legal shortcomings, ensuring ongoing compliance with privacy regulations.

Building a Culture of Data Ethics

Creating a culture that prioritizes data ethics is crucial. This involves ongoing employee training, the establishment of clear data policies, and continuous monitoring and updating of practices to align with the latest laws and standards. Such a culture ensures that ethical data collection becomes ingrained in an organization's DNA.

As technology continues to advance, new methods of data collection will undoubtedly emerge. The challenge for organizations will be to leverage these innovations while maintaining a steadfast commitment to privacy and ethics. Striking this balance is essential for building long-term trust and sustainability in the digital ecosystem.

Conclusion

Web data collection involves a broad spectrum of practices, from harnessing diverse data sources to implementing sophisticated tracking technologies, all while navigating the intricate landscape of privacy and ethics. By mastering these elements, both businesses and individuals can harness the power of web data to inform decision-making, drive innovation, and foster growth in an increasingly data-driven world. Prioritizing data ethics and complying with privacy regulations are not just legal requirements but also integral steps towards building trust with users and ensuring the responsible use of data.

Understanding Web Tagging and UTM Parameters in Google Analytics 4: A Comprehensive Guide

Introduction

In digital analytics, the accurate tracking and analysis of web traffic is paramount. This begins with an understanding of web tagging, a fundamental concept in web analytics. Web tagging involves the placement of code snippets on a website to collect data about visitors and their interactions. In the specific context of Google Analytics 4 (GA4), one of the most vital components of this process involves using Urchin Tracking Module (UTM) parameters. This comprehensive guide delves into the nuances of web tagging, the role of UTM parameters in GA4, and the overarching importance of tagging in the digital landscape.

Web Tagging in Web Analytics

What is Web Tagging?

Web tagging refers to the method of using tags, or small pieces of code, to gather data about the behavior of website visitors. These tags collect several types of information, such as page views, user interactions, and more. This section will cover the basics of web tagging, including its purpose and how it works.

Types of Web Tags

There are several types of web tags, each serving a specific purpose. This includes tags for analytics, conversion tracking, remarketing, and more. An in-depth look at each type of tag and its specific function will provide a clearer understanding of their roles.

Implementation and Best Practices

Implementing web tags correctly is crucial for accurate data collection. This part will discuss the technical aspects of tag implementation, including the use of tag management systems like Google Tag Manager. Additionally, it will cover best practices for tag management and maintenance.

UTM Parameters in Google Analytics 4

Understanding UTM Parameters

UTM parameters are text strings added to URLs to track the effectiveness of online marketing campaigns across traffic sources and publishing media. This section will define UTM parameters and their components: source, medium, campaign, term, and content.

Creating and Using UTM Parameters in GA4

The process of creating UTM parameters for URLs and how these parameters integrate with GA4 will be outlined here. This includes practical examples and step-by-step instructions on setting up UTM parameters for several types of campaigns.

Analyzing Data with UTM Parameters

Once UTM parameters are in place, the next step is analyzing the collected data. This section will guide readers through the process of accessing and interpreting data from UTM parameters in GA4, including the analysis of traffic sources, campaign effectiveness, and user behavior.

The Importance of Tagging in Digital Analytics

Accurate Data Collection

The primary importance of web tagging lies in its ability to accurately collect data. This part will discuss how tagging ensures the collection of reliable and detailed data, which is crucial for any analytics process.

Enhanced User Behavior Understanding

By tracking how users interact with a website, businesses can gain valuable insights into user behavior. This section will explore how tagging can provide deep insights into user engagement, preferences, and conversion paths.

Optimizing Marketing Efforts

With the data collected through tagging, particularly with UTM parameters, marketers can optimize their campaigns. This section will discuss how tagging aids in measuring campaign performance, enabling data-driven decision-making, and leading to improved marketing ROI.

In conclusion, web tagging and the use of UTM parameters in GA4 are indispensable for any business seeking to leverage web analytics for growth. By understanding and effectively implementing these tools, organizations can gather insightful data, leading to more informed decisions and strategic planning. As digital landscapes continue to evolve, the role of precise and comprehensive web tagging will only grow in significance, underlining its crucial role in the success of online endeavors.

2.4 GA4's Approach to User Privacy and Data Compliance

In the contemporary digital landscape, the importance of privacy and data compliance cannot be overstated. With the introduction of Google Analytics 4 (GA4), a significant shift has been observed in how user data is collected, processed, and utilized for advertising purposes. This evolution mirrors the growing global concern over user privacy and the stringent regulations being put in place to safeguard it.

GA4 represents Google's commitment to privacy-first tracking, user data control, and cross-platform measurement. Unlike its predecessors, GA4 does not rely solely on cookies and instead uses a more robust, event-based data model. This model is designed to be flexible in the face of a cookie-less future, ensuring advertisers can continue to gather valuable insights without compromising on user privacy.

One of the cornerstone features of GA4 in terms of privacy is data minimization. GA4 encourages advertisers to collect only the data necessary for their specific goals. This approach aligns with the General Data Protection Regulation (GDPR) and other global privacy laws that advocate for minimal data collection and increased user consent.

Furthermore, GA4 offers enhanced user consent features. Advertisers can customize data collection based on user consent choices, a feature particularly important in regions where consent is legally required, such as the European Union. This ensures that advertisers respect user preferences, enhancing trust and transparency in the process.

Best Practices for Advertisers in the Context of Privacy Laws

In a world where privacy regulations are becoming more stringent, advertisers must adapt to remain compliant while still reaching their marketing objectives. Here are some best practices:

1. **Understand and Comply with Local and Global Privacy Laws:** Advertisers must stay informed about privacy laws such as GDPR in Europe, CCPA in California, and others that may affect their operations. This includes understanding consent requirements, data subject rights, and data breach notification protocols.
2. **Prioritize Transparency and User Consent:** Clearly communicate with users about what data is being collected and for what purpose. Ensure that obtaining consent is an integral part of the user experience on your website or app.
3. **Implement Privacy-by-Design:** Consider privacy at every stage of the advertising campaign lifecycle. This involves data minimization, ensuring data security, and considering the privacy implications of any new marketing strategy.
4. **Regularly Audit and Update Data Practices:** Regular audits of data collection, storage, and processing practices can help identify and mitigate privacy risks. Stay updated with the latest privacy tools and features offered by platforms like GA4.
5. **Educate and Train Your Team:** Ensure that your team understands the importance of data privacy and is familiar with the relevant laws and tools (like GA4) to ensure compliance.

The Future of Advertising Analytics in a Privacy-Focused World

The future of advertising analytics in a privacy-focused world is likely to be shaped by the following trends:

1. **Increased Use of First-Party Data:** With third-party cookies becoming obsolete, there will be a shift towards first-party data. Advertisers will need to find innovative ways to collect and utilize this data while respecting user privacy.
2. **Growth of Privacy-Enhancing Technologies (PETs):** PETs such as differential privacy and federated learning will become more prevalent. These technologies allow for the analysis of user data without compromising individual privacy.

3. **Machine Learning and Predictive Analytics:** The use of AI and machine learning will increase in advertising analytics. These technologies can help in deriving insights from large datasets while adhering to privacy regulations.
4. **Evolution of Consent Management Platforms (CMPs):** CMPs will become more sophisticated, offering better user experiences while ensuring compliance with privacy laws.
5. **Shift Towards Contextual Advertising:** As personal data becomes harder to access, contextual advertising, which targets ads based on the content being consumed rather than user behavior, will see a resurgence.
6. **Development of New Measurement Metrics:** New metrics that respect user privacy will emerge. These might focus more on aggregated and anonymized data, providing insights without infringing on individual privacy.
7. **Cross-Device and Platform Analytics:** With the increase in multi-device usage, cross-platform analytics that respect user privacy will become essential for a holistic view of the customer journey.

Conclusion

The landscape of advertising analytics is undergoing a paradigm shift, moving towards a more privacy-centric approach. Google Analytics 4 is at the forefront of this change, offering tools and features that align with current privacy laws and user expectations. For advertisers, adapting to these changes involves not only compliance with legal requirements but also a commitment to ethical data practices. As we look towards the future, the industry will continue to evolve, with privacy remaining a key consideration in the development of new advertising technologies and strategies. The challenge for advertisers will be to balance effective targeting and personalization with the growing demand for privacy and data protection.

Key Points:

1. Web data collection methods are essential in the digital world for understanding human behavior, market trends, and societal shifts.
2. Comprehensive data sources include websites, e-commerce platforms, social media analytics, APIs, web services, and public/government datasets.
3. Advanced data collection techniques involve sophisticated web scraping, interactive APIs, online surveys and polls, and behavioral data tracking.
4. Web scraping extracts specific information from web pages, while web crawling systematically navigates and indexes the internet.
5. Implementing tracking codes on websites is crucial for gathering data on user behavior, traffic sources, and site interactions.
6. GA4 (Google Analytics 4) emphasizes privacy-first tracking, user data control, and uses an event-based data model suitable for a cookie-less future.
7. Privacy and ethics in data collection are paramount, with regulations like GDPR and CCPA guiding practices.
8. Web tagging and UTM parameters in GA4 are vital for accurate tracking and analysis of web traffic.
9. Advertisers must adapt to stringent privacy regulations and ethical data practices while effectively reaching marketing objectives.
10. The future of advertising analytics is shifting towards privacy-focused approaches, with an emphasis on first-party data and privacy-enhancing technologies.

Discussion Questions:

1. How do advanced web scraping and web crawling methods differ in their approach to data collection, and what are their unique applications?
2. What are the challenges and considerations involved in implementing advanced tracking codes on websites?
3. How does GA4's approach to user privacy and data compliance differ from previous versions of Google Analytics?
4. In what ways can organizations ensure they are adhering to international privacy laws like GDPR and CCPA while collecting web data?
5. What future trends in advertising analytics are likely to emerge as the industry shifts towards a more privacy-centric approach?

Chapter Three: Web Metrics

3.1 Introduction

In the digital age, where data is often considered the new oil, the importance of web analytics in shaping business strategies and online experiences cannot be overstated. However, the true power of web analytics does not solely reside in the sheer volume of data collected but in the astuteness of selecting and focusing on the right metrics. This chapter delves into the criticality of establishing the right web metrics, guiding businesses and analysts through the intricate process of identifying metrics that align with specific business objectives and digital strategies.

The landscape of web analytics is vast and varied, offering a multitude of metrics – from page views and session duration to conversion rates and customer lifetime value. Each of these metrics can provide valuable insights, but not all will be relevant to every business or scenario. The challenge, therefore, lies in discerning which metrics are most pertinent to your specific goals. Are you looking to increase brand awareness, boost online sales, enhance customer engagement, or improve customer retention? The answer to this question shapes the choice of metrics, turning data into actionable insights and strategies into results.

Moreover, the selection of the right web metric is not just a matter of relevance; it is also about precision and depth. In a world inundated with data, it is easy to get lost in the noise. Key performance indicators (KPIs) need to be precisely defined to ensure that they provide the insights needed to make informed decisions. This precision in metric selection requires a deep understanding of the business's online ecosystem, the behavior of its target audience, and the dynamics of the digital market.

The impact of choosing the right metric extends beyond mere measurement; it influences the strategic direction of a business. A well-chosen metric can illuminate pathways to optimization, highlight areas in need of improvement, and reveal opportunities for growth. It is a beacon guiding businesses through the complex and ever-changing digital landscape, ensuring that every step taken is one in the right direction.

This chapter aims to unravel the complexities of web metric selection, providing a comprehensive guide on identifying and implementing the most effective metrics for your web analytics initiatives. Through this exploration, readers will gain insights into aligning metrics with business objectives, understanding user behavior, and ultimately, harnessing the power of data to drive successful online strategies.

3.2 Fundamentals of Metrics

There exists a plethora of methods for determining the effectiveness of a marketing campaign, e.g., page visits, bounce rate, opens, clicks, cost-per-opportunity, and return on investment (ROI). It is important to establish the metrics of progress when planning a marketing strategy in order to meet corporate objectives. Marketing teams leverage metrics and key performance indicators (KPIs) to manage those campaigns and digital experiences. In establishing the correct metrics, the team can ensure its ability to accurately measure how well those campaigns resonate with the target audience.

Metrics help define all aspects of digital strategy. From vision setting to planning and implementation, one key thread across all phases of a strategy is the metric used by the digital marketer to establish performance standards. Metrics can influence and define new strategies or spark a resurgence or renewed effort of a preexisting strategy. Generally, this is all contingent on how effectively the metrics are established by the digital strategist. For all of these reasons, the strategists' ability to determine appropriate metrics is crucial.

They first need to ask themselves what the goal of the digital strategy is. The corresponding answer must reflect a direct, impactful outcome. That business impact can be qualitative or quantitative in nature and should have some level of value for both the organization itself and its customers. It is sufficient that the established metric simply identifies a value, i.e., it need not have equal impact on both parties.

What is a Good Metric?

According to Shah (2013), movement and company goals are the two main concepts of note. When it comes to analytics, we should not focus on reporting simply for the sake of reporting. Instead, we should concern ourselves with monitoring true progress. Metrics establish the movement of users and how they navigate their digital journeys. They should evaluate how user digital experiences are being created for strategic company goals and objectives. With that in mind, here is how we define a "good metric."

A good metric is

- **Comparative**. Comparing a metric over time and across user groups or competitors reveals the direction in which trends are heading. An example of this is comparing one segment of users to another, such as an older and a younger generation. This metric will establish if one age group engages with the digital strategy more than the other.

- **Understandable.** For example, imagine that an analyst has taken the numbers they have been monitoring (the ones believed to be the most important) and has shown them to their business partners. If they fail to understand the analyst's intent with these metrics, then the figures being monitored are probably too complicated. Internally, if people cannot remember and freely discuss the analytics of interest based off the chosen metrics, it will be far more difficult to transform a data shift into a profit.

- **A ratio or rate.** Ratios and rates, which can establish trends, have a comparative value in their measurement. Trend analysis is a critical type of analysis used in digital analytics that showcases the moments happening over a period time. Generally speaking, in digital strategies and marketing, the goal of the organization is to increase trends in an intended direction. Ratios and rates (unlike absolute numbers) offer a more realistic "health check" for a business and, as a result, are easier to act on. A ratio, for example, could be the evaluation of the number of website visits per user over a specific time period. If one hundred users visit a website for a total of 1,000 visits, then the ratio works out to 1:10, i.e., on average, every user visited the website ten times (Sponder & Khan, 2018).

- **Behavior Changing**. Essentially, we wish to understand whether the strategy implemented is driving the influence and action based on the corporate goals. The metric should help decision markers determine what works and what does not. It should clearly determine whether the behavior of the consumer is moving in the direction needed to ensure optimal value in the strategic outcome.

- **Benchmarked** A benchmark establishes an industry-wide score for which companies within that same industry would strive. It reflects a particular metric's average performance and, thus, the performance of the company at large. To ensure that benchmarks are worth implementing, a company could track its own metrics over a period of time.

- **Controllable**. The strategist must recognize whether the metric established could be changed due to management influence (or any other consideration). Metrics must generally be controlled in an effort to measure effective performance of the strategic goals. One example of this is website traffic growth as opposed to internet growth: The growth of website traffic can evolve based on how strategies are shifted and, because it is countable, is considered controllable. By comparison, the traffic's impact on other metrics could be viewed as uncontrollable.

- **Relevant.** The metrics established for a company's strategy should be relevant to that company. The metric should align with the strategic objective of the organization and establish credibility for the strategy's justification. For example, one could measure overall sales against the sales contributions gained from a particular advertising campaign. In this scenario, if we want to understand the impact of a specific campaign, then we measure its sales performance.

Overall, what defines a "good metric" truly depends on the strategy at hand. Nevertheless, it should, to some extent, reflect the elements provided above. Without any of them, the metric established will not drive further value or garner results for the digital strategist.

Leading Metrics versus Lagging Metrics

Both leading and lagging metrics are important in their intended areas of application. We must determine if the tactic being monitored is helping us make smart choices at a fast pace, bearing in mind that a true metric must be actionable. By comparison, leading metrics make predictions about the future, i.e., they offer an insight into what is expected to happen. A leading metric often correlates with predictive digital analytics. Hemann and Burbary (2018) state that predictive analytics uses data, mathematical

algorithms, and machine learning approaches to evaluate the likelihood of possible outcomes based on previously existing data. Rather than simply comprehending what has occurred, the goal is to have the most accurate forecast of what will occur in the future, e.g., concerning the direction of currents trend. Data analysts can use predictive modeling in statistical software to generate such insights.

According to Hemann and Burbary (2018), the ability to predict how successful a marketing campaign will be is beneficial to any organization. Predictive modeling is direct in its use of artificial intelligence to help formulate predictions in the marketing field. Through the use of artificial intelligence (AI), digital analysts can work toward those leading metrics if they must be established; conversely, AI can lean on this metric from the start to provide a predicted outcome. It is important to remember that metrics can be either explored or expected.

Correlated versus Causal Metrics

Metrics often support other measurements of performance and other metrics. At times, one metric must be evaluated before another can be established. When two metrics appear to change in conjunction with one another, but are profoundly changing due to a secondary factor, we call this a correlative relationship. For example, customer acquisition and customer retention are relevant to one another: customer acquisition focuses on obtaining new customers to conduct business with the company; customer retention focuses on ensuring repeated business with the same customers over time. Their correlation lies in the fact that any given customer data used for customer acquisition can later become relevant as retention data, i.e., the same data can simply be processed in diverse ways (Madhavan, 2019).

Causations, by comparison, are discovered by defining an association and then conducting experiments on it to measure any variance. They are not direct relationships, and several variables can be at play here. Causality, although difficult to master, is considered a superpower in analytics, as it allows a digital strategy to optimize future trends and outcomes. In fact, even a glimpse into the level of causality present in the data can be rather helpful. Generally speaking, finding correlations and connections across metrics is key to analytics and bolsters the strategist's ability to make accurate predictions (Madhavan, 2019).

Behavioral and Financial Metrics—The Perfect Combination

Digital strategy is focused on driving two specific types of value and benefits to a company, which take the form of behavioral and financial metrics. Behavioral metrics offer insight into user interaction with marketing content, user experience, and user behavior. They let us see, e.g., what customers are doing, where they are going, and what their preferences are. This crucial information aids the marketing team in developing content, campaigns, and messages to enhance the digital experiences. Other important behavioral metrics that need to be established include those which evaluate the intent and motivation of the user. Digital strategy considers how the user experience can be optimized to influence their behavior to drive an action or conversion. Understanding the user's attitude toward that experience, as well as their preferred methods of communication and interaction, is essential when using combined financial metrics in digital analytics.

Financial metrics measure how well a digital campaign (or experience) drives revenue and brings profitability to the organization. Digital strategies should influence behavior to where it contributes to the bottom-line financial metrics. This behavior directly reflects the organization's fiscal health.

The ideal digital strategy makes use of both financial and behavioral metrics and understands how to best combine and measure them, thereby distilling them into one single perspective. In other words, how are the behavioral techniques driving financial performance? Ultimately, metrics follow the digital funnel paradigm, where the organization in question grabs the customer's attention, steers them toward an end point, establishes the user experience, and pushes the customer to take action. Each step of the behavioral metrics funnel ultimately leads to a last action point, where the financial metric is evaluated. Essentially, the two work in tandem within a digital strategy to drive and measure the ultimate performance.

3.3 Traffic Metrics

In-Depth Analysis of Traffic Sources

Traffic metrics are fundamental in assessing the volume and source of website visitors, offering vital clues about the site's visibility and the effectiveness of various marketing channels.

1. **Unique Visitors:**
    - **Definition:** Counts distinct individuals visiting a site within a specified timeframe.
    - **Example Calculation:** If five hundred different users visit a site in a day, the number of unique visitors for that day is 500.
    - **Application:** Essential for understanding the website's reach and audience size.
2. **Page Views:**
    - **Definition:** The total number of pages viewed, including repeated views of a single page.
    - **Example Calculation:** If a user visits three pages, it counts as three page views.

- **Application:** Useful in determining the overall engagement level with the site's content.

3. **Traffic Sources:**
   - **Definition:** Classifies traffic into categories like direct, referral, organic search, and social.
   - **Example Calculation:** If 40% of traffic comes from search engines, 30% from direct visits, 20% from referrals, and 10% from social media, these percentages represent the traffic source distribution.
   - **Application:** Helps in understanding where the audience is coming from and where to focus marketing efforts.

4. **Bounce Rate:**
   - **Definition:** The percentage of visitors who leave the site after viewing only one page.
   - **Example Calculation:** If 100 users visit a site and 50 leave after only one page, the bounce rate is 50%.
   - **Application:** Indicates whether the landing pages are effectively engaging or relevant to the visitors.

5. **Average Session Duration:**
   - **Definition:** The average amount of time spent by a visitor in a session.
   - **Example Calculation:** If 5 users spend 10, 15, 20, 5, and 10 minutes respectively, the average session duration is (10+15+20+5+10)/5 = 12 minutes.
   - **Application:** Longer durations typically indicate higher engagement levels.

3.4 Engagement Metrics

Deep Dive into User Interaction

Engagement metrics reveal how visitors interact with a website, indicating the effectiveness of content and usability.

1. **Pages per Session:**
   - **Definition:** The average number of pages viewed during a session.
   - **Example Calculation:** If a visitor views 3 pages in one session and another views 5 in another, the average is (3+5)/2 = 4 pages per session.

- **Application:** More pages per session suggest engaging content and a well-structured website.

2. **Average Time on Page:**
   - **Definition:** Shows the average time spent by visitors on a specific page.
   - **Example Calculation:** If one user spends 2 minutes on a page and another spends 4 minutes, the average time on the page is (2+4)/2 = 3 minutes.
   - **Application:** Useful in assessing content relevance and engagement on individual pages.

3. **Event Tracking:**
   - **Definition:** Tracks specific interactions on a page, like downloads or video plays.
   - **Example Calculation:** If a video is played 100 times in a day, the event count for that action is 100.
   - **Application:** Provides detailed insights into how users interact with specific elements.

4. **Scroll Depth:**
   - **Definition:** Measures how far down the page users scroll.
   - **Example Calculation:** If the average scroll depth on a page is 75%, it means most users scroll through three-quarters of the page content.
   - **Application:** Deeper scroll depths imply compelling content that retains user interest.

3.5 Conversion Metrics

Evaluating Effectiveness in Achieving Goals

Conversion metrics are critical in gauging how well a website prompts visitors to take a desired action, reflecting directly on the site's success in achieving its business objectives.

1. **Conversion Rate:**
   - **Definition:** The percentage of visitors who complete a desired action.
   - **Example Calculation:** If 1,000 visitors come to a site and 50 make a purchase, the conversion rate is (50/1000) *100 = 5%.
   - **Application:** Directly measures the effectiveness of the website in achieving conversion goals.

2. **Cost per Conversion:**
    - **Definition:** Indicates the cost-effectiveness of converting a visitor into a customer, crucial for paid campaigns.
    - **Example Calculation:** If a campaign costs $1000 and generates 50 conversions, the cost per conversion is $1000/50 = $20.
    - **Application:** Vital for assessing the financial efficiency of marketing strategies.
3. **Funnel Analysis:**
    - **Definition:** Examines the steps a user takes before completing a conversion.
    - **Example Calculation:** In a four-step funnel, if 1000 enter the first step and only 50 complete the final conversion, the funnel conversion rate is 50/1000 = 5%.
    - **Application:** Helps identify potential drop-off points and bottlenecks.
4. **Goal Completion:**
    - **Definition:** Tracks the total number of times a specific goal is achieved.
    - **Example Calculation:** If the goal is newsletter sign-ups and 100 users sign up in a week, the goal completion for that week is 100.
    - **Application:** Direct measure of specific objectives being met, such as sign-ups or downloads.

3.6 Retention Metrics

Gauging Long-Term User Engagement and Value

Retention metrics assess a website's ability to maintain its visitor base over time, indicating customer loyalty and long-term value.

1. **Return Visitor Rate:**
    - **Definition:** The percentage of visitors who return to the site.
    - **Example Calculation:** If 200 out of 500 total visitors are returning visitors, the return visitor rate is (200/500) *100 = 40%.
    - **Application:** High rates suggest strong content or product loyalty.
2. **Frequency and Recency of Visits:**
    - **Definition:** Tracks how often and how recently visitors return to the site.

- **Example Calculation:** If an average visitor returns twice a month, the frequency is two visits per month.
- **Application:** Provides insights into user habits and loyalty.

3. **Customer Lifetime Value (CLV):**
    - **Definition:** The total revenue expected from a single customer account over time.
    - **Example Calculation:** If a customer spends an average of $50 per visit and visits 20 times over their 'lifetime', the CLV is 20*$50 = $1000.
    - **Application:** Helps understand the long-term value of customer relationships.
4. **Churn Rate:**
    - **Definition:** The rate at which customers stop doing business with the site.
    - **Example Calculation:** If 10 out of 100 subscribers cancel in a month, the churn rate is (10/100) *100 = 10%.
    - **Application:** Critical for subscription-based models, indicating customer retention effectiveness.

Choosing the Right Metric for the Right Scenario

Tailoring Metrics to Business Goals

The selection of the right metric depends heavily on the specific goals and context of the website. Here are some guidelines:

1. **For Increasing Traffic:** Focus on traffic metrics like unique visitors and traffic sources. They help in understanding audience size and the effectiveness of different channels in driving traffic.
2. **For Enhancing User Engagement:** Engagement metrics like pages per session and average time on page are key. They provide insights into how engaging and relevant the content is to the audience.
3. **For Boosting Sales or Conversions:** Conversion rate and cost per conversion are crucial. They offer a direct measure of the effectiveness of the website and marketing campaigns in driving sales or other desired actions.
4. **For Improving Customer Loyalty:** Retention metrics like return visitor rate and CLV are important. They help in understanding how well the site retains customers and the long-term value they bring.

Case Examples

Here are three use case examples using real company names to illustrate how they might choose the right metric for their specific web analysis needs:

1. **E-commerce Website: Increasing Sales Conversion**

   Company: Zara, a global fashion retailer.

   Objective: To increase online sales.

   Chosen Metric: Conversion Rate.

   Rationale: For Zara, with its extensive online presence, monitoring the conversion rate is crucial. This metric measures the percentage of website visitors who make a purchase. By focusing on this metric, Zara can understand how effectively its website converts browsing into buying. This insight is critical for assessing the performance of its online catalog, the impact of digital marketing campaigns, and the user-friendliness of the checkout process. Strategies to improve the conversion rate might include optimizing product pages, offering targeted promotions, and simplifying the online shopping process.

2. **B2B Service Provider: Lead Generation**

   Company: Salesforce, a leader in customer relationship management (CRM) software.

   Objective: To generate more qualified leads.

   Chosen Metric: Lead Conversion Rate.

   Rationale: For Salesforce, generating high-quality leads is essential for business growth. The lead conversion rate, which is the percentage of visitors who engage in a way that classifies them as a lead (such as filling out a contact form or signing up for a trial), is a vital metric. It helps Salesforce gauge the effectiveness of its website in capturing the interest of potential clients. Focusing on this metric allows Salesforce to tailor its online content, refine its calls-to-action, and improve lead magnets like demos or informational webinars, aiming to attract and convert potential customers.

3. **Content Publisher: Enhancing User Engagement**

   Company: The New York Times, a leading news provider.

   Objective: To increase user engagement and session duration.

   Chosen Metric: Average Time on Page and Pages per Session.

   Rationale: For The New York Times, which operates a successful online news platform, user engagement is key, especially as it relates to ad revenue. Metrics like average time on page and pages per session are crucial for understanding how engaging and compelling their content is to readers. These insights allow The New York Times to identify which types of articles keep readers on the site longer and encourage them to explore more content. Improving on these metrics can lead to increased ad impressions and, consequently, higher advertising revenue.

In each case, the selected metric directly supports the company's overarching business goals, providing focused insights to inform targeted improvements and strategic decision-making.

Conclusion

Understanding and effectively utilizing key metrics in web analytics is vital for any website aiming to optimize its performance. Each metric offers unique insights, from traffic and engagement to conversions and retention. By choosing the right metrics based on specific business objectives and scenarios, websites can make data-driven decisions to enhance their user experience, achieve their goals, and drive sustainable growth.

This expanded and detailed chapter provides a comprehensive look at key metrics in web analytics, complete with example calculations for each metric and guidance on selecting appropriate metrics for different web analysis scenarios.

Key Points:

1. The effectiveness of web analytics hinges on selecting and focusing on the right metrics that align with specific business objectives and digital strategies.
2. Identifying pertinent metrics involves understanding the business's goals, such as increasing brand awareness, boosting sales, enhancing customer engagement, or improving retention.
3. Precision in metric selection requires a deep understanding of the business's online ecosystem, target audience behavior, and digital market dynamics.
4. A well-chosen metric influences the strategic direction of a business, highlighting pathways for optimization, areas needing improvement, and growth opportunities.
5. Good metrics should be comparative, understandable, a ratio or rate, behavior-changing, benchmarked, controllable, and relevant.
6. Differentiating between leading and lagging metrics, as well as correlated and causal metrics, is crucial in digital strategy formulation.
7. Combining behavioral and financial metrics is essential for a comprehensive digital strategy, reflecting both user interactions and financial impact.
8. Traffic metrics, such as unique visitors, page views, traffic sources, bounce rate, and average session duration, are fundamental for assessing website visibility and marketing effectiveness.
9. Engagement metrics, including pages per session, average time on page, event tracking, and scroll depth, reveal user interaction levels, and content effectiveness.
10. Conversion metrics like conversion rate, cost per conversion, funnel analysis, and goal completion are key in evaluating a website's success in achieving its objectives.
11. Retention metrics, such as return visitor rate, frequency and recency of visits, customer lifetime value (CLV), and churn rate, gauge long-term user engagement and value.

Discussion Questions:

1. How does the selection of web analytics metrics influence the development and success of digital marketing strategies?
2. What considerations should be made when choosing between behavioral and financial metrics in web analytics?
3. How can businesses effectively balance the use of leading and lagging metrics to predict future trends and measure past performance?
4. In what ways can engagement metrics like average time on page and pages per session inform content strategy and website design?
5. How do retention metrics like CLV and churn rate help businesses understand long-term customer value and loyalty?

Chapter Four: Web Analytics Tools

4.1 Introduction

In digital marketing and website management, web analytics tools play a pivotal role. They are sophisticated software solutions designed to track, analyze, and report on website data. This data encompasses a range of metrics, from user behavior and traffic sources to conversions and engagement. The choice of the right web analytics tool is crucial as it can significantly impact a company's ability to understand its online presence, make data-driven decisions, and optimize its digital strategy.

The importance of selecting the right tool lies in its ability to provide relevant insights tailored to specific business needs. Different tools offer varying features, ranging from basic traffic analysis to complex user journey mapping. The choice should align with the company's size, industry, specific goals, and technical capabilities.

Google Analytics 4

Overview

Google Analytics 4 (GA4) is the latest iteration of Google's popular web analytics service. It offers a more user-centric approach to tracking, utilizing machine learning to provide insights and predictive metrics.

Key Features

- **Event-Based Tracking:** Unlike its predecessor, GA4 focuses on event-based data, allowing for more flexible and comprehensive tracking.
- **Cross-Platform Tracking:** GA4 enables tracking across websites and apps, providing a unified view of the user journey.
- **Predictive Analytics:** Utilizes machine learning to predict future user actions, such as potential revenue from specific customer segments.

Best Use Cases

GA4 is ideal for businesses seeking an advanced, integrated view of their user interactions across different platforms and devices.

Adobe Analytics

Overview

Adobe Analytics is a part of the Adobe Experience Cloud, offering powerful analytics capabilities for enterprise-level businesses and marketers.

Key Features

- **Segmentation:** Advanced user segmentation capabilities to analyze specific groups of visitors.
- **Real-Time Analytics:** Provides real-time data, allowing businesses to make quick, informed decisions.
- **Multichannel Data Collection:** Collects data from various channels, including online, offline, mobile, and more.

Best Use Cases

Adobe Analytics is best suited for large enterprises requiring deep, real-time insights across various channels and touchpoints.

Hotjar

Overview

Hotjar is a behavior analytics tool that offers a more qualitative approach, focusing on how users interact with a website.

Key Features

- **Heatmaps:** Visual representation of where users click, move, and scroll on a site.
- **Session Recordings:** Records user sessions to provide insights into user behavior and experience.
- **Feedback Tools:** Allows collection of direct user feedback through polls and surveys.

Best Use Cases

Hotjar is particularly useful for UX/UI designers and website managers looking to understand user behavior and improve site usability.

Mixpanel

Overview

Mixpanel specializes in user analytics, helping businesses track user interactions and measure the effectiveness of product changes.

Key Features

- **Event Tracking:** Tracks user interactions with specific elements on a website or app.
- **Funnel Analysis:** Analyzes user journey through specific paths, identifying drop-off points.
- **A/B Testing:** Tests different versions of a product to determine which performs better.

Best Use Cases

Mixpanel is ideal for product managers and digital marketers focused on user engagement and retention in web and mobile applications.

4.2 Google Analytics 4 vs Adobe Analytics

While we did introduce several web analytics tools, the top two that really have the largest market share of use in organizations is Google Analytics 4 or Adobe Analytics. It is important to understand the usage, similarities, and differences between the two in how organizations make their decisions on which tool to adopt. The reason this is important is because of a few key reasons:

1) The investment of a web analytics tool is expensive
2) It generates the type of analytics and insights the company chooses to use in their strategic planning
3) It is not easy to just pivot, it takes time to develop data connections, establish user controls, build a framework of use cases and more

Therefore, the vetting and decision process of evaluation is critical.

According to W3Techs.com: As of December 2023, the usage and market share of Google Analytics compared to Adobe Analytics reveal interesting trends in the industry. Google Analytics is used by 54.1% of all websites, translating to a traffic analysis tool market share of 84.4%. In contrast,

Adobe Analytics has a much smaller footprint, with only 0.1% of websites using it, equating to a 0.2% market share. However, it is important to note that the market share of Adobe Analytics increases to 5% among the top 1,000 websites, indicating its popularity in high-traffic, enterprise-level environments

Both Google Analytics and Adobe Analytics have their unique strengths and are integrated with their respective marketing stacks. Google Analytics is known for its integration with the Google Marketing Platform, including tools like Campaign Manager 360 and Google Optimize, making it highly beneficial for website optimization and digital media. Adobe Analytics, on the other hand, integrates with the Adobe Experience Cloud ecosystem, offering advanced tools for personalized marketing campaigns and customer experience optimization.

In terms of customization and data analysis, Adobe Analytics is often considered more flexible and customizable, especially in data visualization and reporting. It allows for extensive options in data analysis, including advanced segmentation and attribution modeling. Google Analytics, while offering a range of customization features, is generally regarded as less flexible compared to Adobe Analytics but is valued for its user-friendly interface and easier implementation.

When choosing between these two platforms, businesses need to consider their specific requirements, technical expertise, and budget. Google Analytics is widely adopted due to its user-friendly interface and free version, making it accessible for businesses of all sizes. Adobe Analytics, with its advanced features and customization options, is more suited for enterprise-level organizations that require deeper data analysis and more sophisticated marketing strategies.

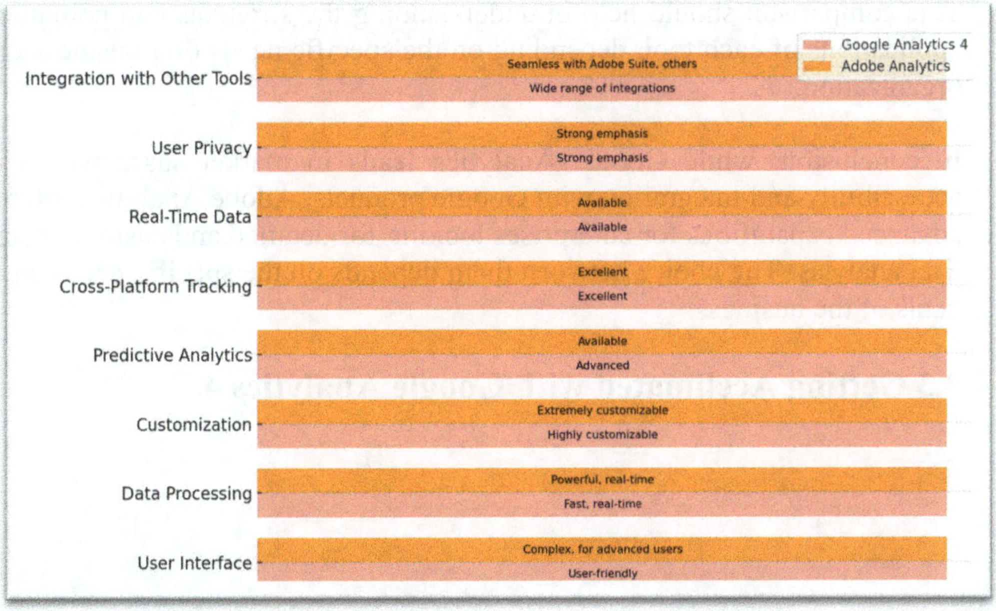

Figure 4.1 Google Analytics 4 vs Adobe Analytics

The above is a chart comparing Google Analytics 4 (GA4) and Adobe Analytics across various features. This comparison should provide a clear overview of the key differences and similarities between these two prominent web analytics tools:

- **User Interface:** GA4 offers a user-friendly interface, while Adobe Analytics is more complex, catering to advanced users.
- **Data Processing:** Both provide fast, real-time data processing capabilities.
- **Customization:** Both tools offer high levels of customization, with Adobe Analytics noted for its extremely customizable nature.
- **Predictive Analytics:** Advanced predictive analytics are available in GA4, and Adobe Analytics also includes predictive features.
- **Cross-Platform Tracking:** Both tools excel in cross-platform tracking capabilities.
- **Real-Time Data:** Real-time data analysis is available in both GA4 and Adobe Analytics.
- **User Privacy:** Both platforms place a strong emphasis on user privacy.
- **Integration with Other Tools:** GA4 offers a wide range of integrations, while Adobe Analytics provides seamless integration with the Adobe Suite and other tools.

This comparison should help in understanding the strengths and potential applications of each tool, depending on the specific needs of a business or organization.

In conclusion, while Google Analytics leads in market share with its accessibility and integration with Google products, Adobe Analytics offers advanced capabilities for enterprises looking for detailed and customizable data analysis. The choice between them depends on the specific needs and goals of the business.

4.3 Getting Acclimated with Google Analytics 4

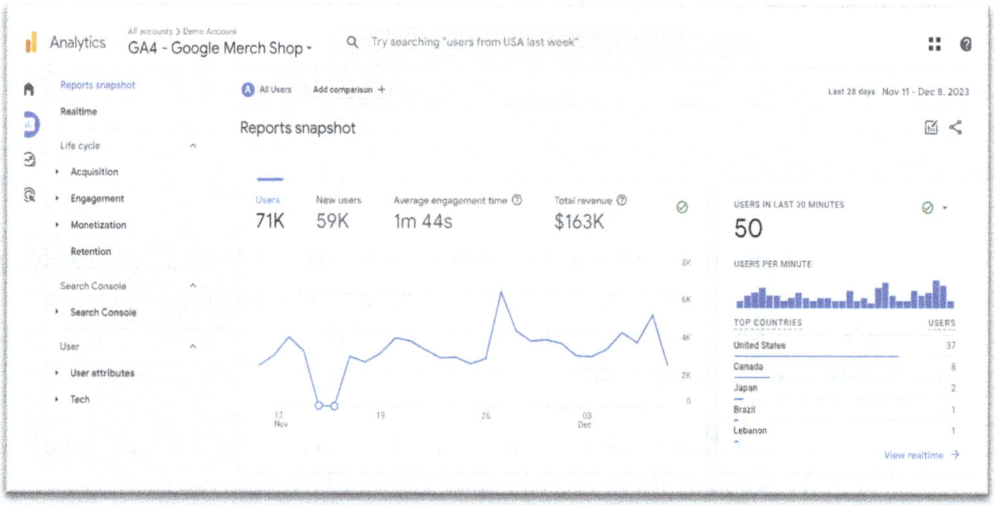

Figure 4.2 Google Analytics Default View

Understanding Google Analytics 4 (GA4)

Google Analytics 4 represents a significant shift from its predecessor, Universal Analytics. This latest version is designed to provide a more comprehensive understanding of customer behavior across websites and apps. GA4 is built on the foundation of privacy, flexibility, and cross-platform measurement, catering to the evolving digital landscape.

Key Changes in Google Analytics 4

1. **Event-Driven Data Model:** Unlike Universal Analytics, which was session-based, GA4 uses an event-driven data model. This model offers more flexibility in tracking user interactions, providing richer insights into user behavior.

2. **Cross-Platform Tracking:** GA4 allows for the seamless integration of data across websites and mobile apps. This unified view helps in understanding the complete customer journey.
3. **Focus on User Privacy:** In response to increasing privacy concerns, GA4 has enhanced privacy features, including cookieless measurement and data deletion controls.
4. **Predictive Analytics:** Utilizing machine learning, GA4 offers predictive insights, such as potential revenue from various customer segments.
5. **Enhanced Reporting and Analysis:** GA4 comes with a new interface for reporting and analysis, offering more customization options and insights.

Navigating the Main Functions of Google Analytics 4

Setting Up and Configuring GA4

- **Account Creation:** Setting up a GA4 account involves creating a property and configuring data streams for your website or app.
- **Event Tracking:** In GA4, events track user interactions. You can use predefined events or create custom events based on your specific needs.

Understanding Reports in GA4

- **Real-time Report:** Provides immediate insights into user activity on your site or app.
- **Life Cycle Reports:** These reports offer insights into the customer journey, covering acquisition, engagement, monetization, and retention.
- **User Exploration:** An advanced analysis tool that allows for the exploration of user data based on various segments and metrics.

Key Analysis Techniques

- **Analysis Hub:** This feature offers a workspace for deep analysis using various techniques, including path analysis and funnel analysis.
- **Audience Building:** GA4 allows you to create custom audiences based on user behavior, which can be used for targeted marketing.

Transitioning from Universal Analytics to GA4

- **Migrating Data:** It is important to note that historical data from Universal Analytics cannot be transferred to GA4. Hence, it is crucial to run both platforms in parallel for a period to collect historical data in GA4.

Utilizing GA4 for Strategic Insights

- **Leveraging Predictive Metrics:** Use GA4's predictive metrics to forecast future trends and customer actions.
- **Custom Dashboards:** Create custom dashboards for a tailored view of your data, focusing on metrics that matter most to your business.

Detailed Exploration of Lifecycle Sections in Google Analytics 4 (GA4)

Acquisition

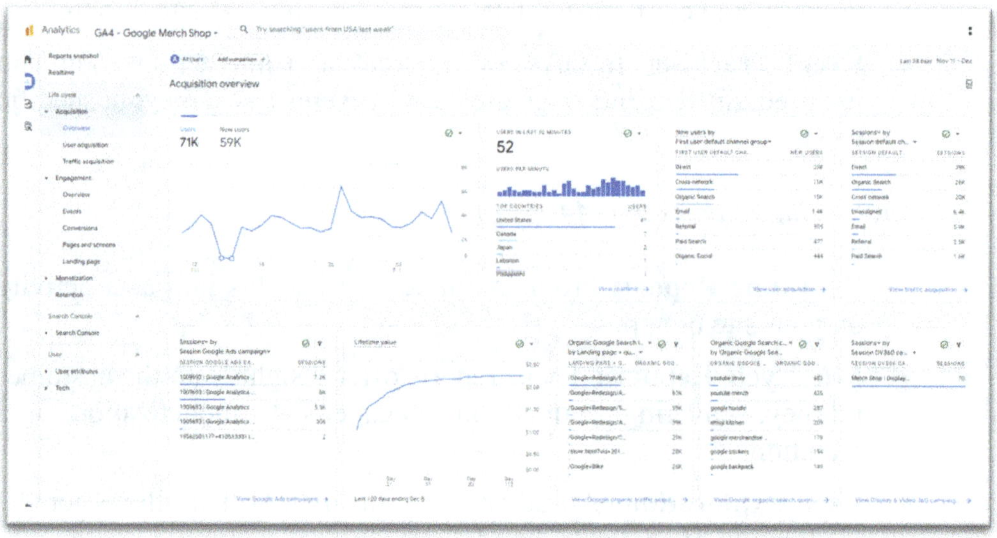

Figure 4.3 Google Analytics 4 Acquisition View

Deep Dive into User Acquisition Analysis

- **User Acquisition Report:** This report shows how new users discover your site or app. It is essential for understanding the initial touchpoints of the user journey. Metrics like 'New Users by Channel' and 'New Users by Source/Medium' provide insights into which channels are most effective in attracting new users.

- **Traffic Acquisition Report:** It gives a broader view of all traffic sources, not just new users. This report is vital for evaluating the overall effectiveness of marketing strategies across various channels.

Application of Acquisition Data

- Utilize acquisition data to identify the most effective marketing channels for attracting new users.
- Adjust marketing budgets and strategies based on the performance of different acquisition channels.

Engagement

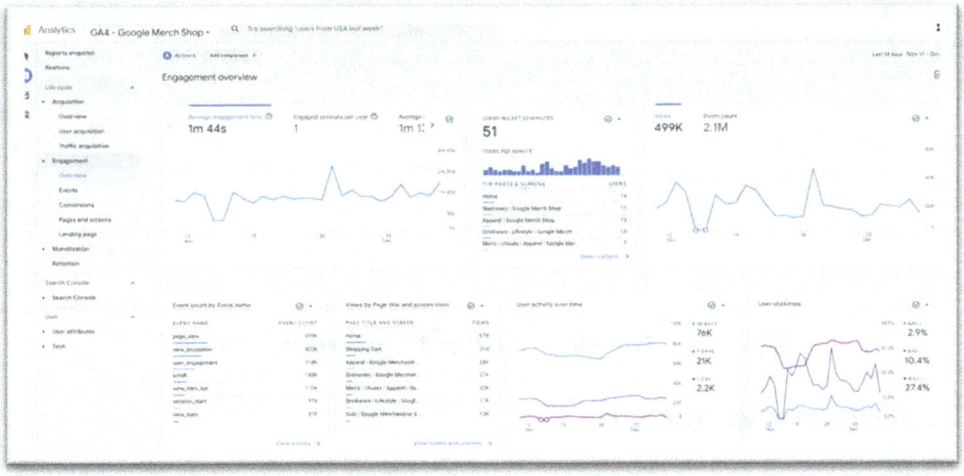

Figure 4.4 Google Analytics 4 Engagement View

In-Depth Analysis of User Engagement

- **Engagement Overview Report:** Offers a snapshot of user engagement metrics like engagement rate, engagement time, and event count. This overview is crucial for gauging the general interest of users in your site or app.
- **Events Report:** Provides details on specific interactions within your site or app. Custom events can be set up to track virtually any user interaction, giving a granular view of how users interact with your content.

Utilizing Engagement Insights

- Identify which content or features are capturing user interest and driving engagement.
- Develop strategies to increase user interaction based on insights from event tracking.

Monetization

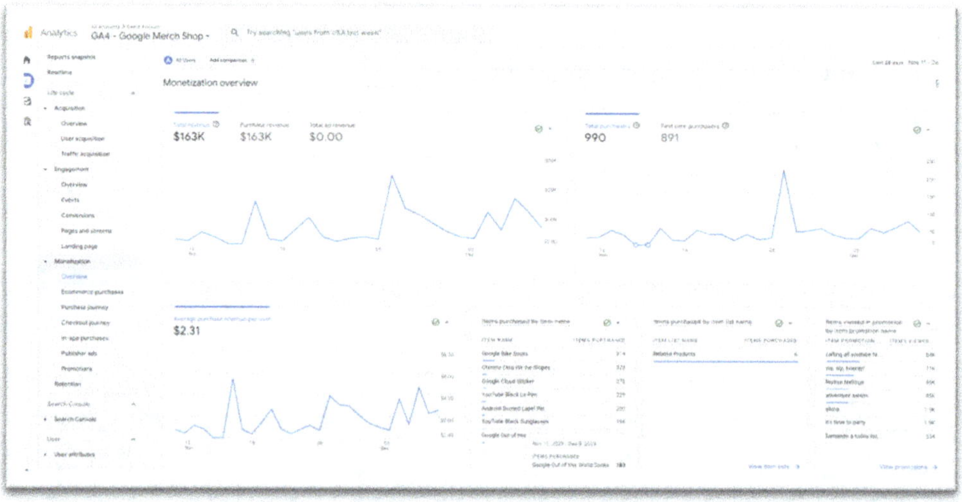

Figure 4.5 Google Analytics 4 Monetization View

Detailed Revenue Analysis

- **Revenue Analysis Report:** Tracks revenue generation in detail, breaking down revenue sources such as e-commerce transactions or in-app purchases.
- **E-commerce Purchase Funnel Report:** Offers a step-by-step analysis of the e-commerce funnel, showing where users enter and exit the purchase process.

Optimizing Revenue Streams

- Analyze revenue patterns to identify opportunities for increasing sales and overall revenue.
- Use funnel analysis to pinpoint and address drop-off points in the e-commerce process.

Retention

Figure 4.6 Google Analytics 4 Retention View

Comprehensive Retention Tracking

- **User Retention Report:** Shows how well your site or app retains users after their first visit. This report is crucial for understanding long-term user engagement.
- **Cohort Analysis Report:** Breaks down user data into cohorts based on shared characteristics or experiences. This analysis is invaluable for tracking the behavior of specific user groups over time.

Enhancing User Retention

- Use retention data to develop strategies for increasing return visits and long-term user engagement.
- Apply insights from cohort analysis to tailor user experience for different segments.

Search Console

Figure 4.7 Google Analytics 4 Search Console View

The integration of Google Search Console (GSC) with Google Analytics 4 (GA4) offers a powerful tool for understanding how your website performs in Google Search and how this relates to your overall website traffic. This detailed overview of the Search Console function in GA4 will cover its key aspects and utility.

Purpose of Google Search Console in GA4

Google Search Console provides insights into how your website is seen and indexed by Google Search, which can greatly influence your site's traffic and performance. The integration with GA4 allows you to analyze and correlate this data with your overall web analytics, offering a comprehensive view of your online presence.

Key Features of Search Console in GA4

1. **Search Performance Data:** You can view data from GSC directly in GA4, which includes metrics such as clicks, impressions, click-through rate (CTR), and the average position of your website in search results.
2. **Query and Page Analysis:** The integration allows you to see which search queries (keywords) and pages are driving traffic to your site. This can be critical in understanding your site's visibility in search and how users are finding you.
3. **User Behavior Insights:** By linking GSC with GA4, you can analyze how users who arrive via organic search interact with your

website compared to other traffic sources. This includes insights into user engagement, conversion rates, and more.

4. **Geographical Performance:** Search Console data in GA4 can help you understand how well your site performs in different geographic locations, offering insights for localized marketing strategies.

Benefits of Using Search Console with GA4

- **SEO Optimization:** By understanding the search queries leading to your site, you can optimize your content and SEO strategies for better search engine rankings and performance.
- **Content Strategy Development:** Insights into popular pages and queries can inform your content strategy, helping you to focus on topics that are more likely to drive traffic.
- **Holistic View of Traffic Sources:** Integrating GSC data into GA4 provides a more complete picture of your traffic sources, allowing for better-informed decisions about marketing and web development strategies.

Setting Up Search Console in GA4

To use Search Console data in GA4, you first need to link your GSC account to your GA4 property. This can usually be done in the GA4 interface under the Admin settings, where you can connect to your GSC account and select the relevant data to be imported.

The Search Console function in GA4 is a vital tool for any website owner or marketer looking to enhance their website's performance in Google Search. By offering detailed insights into search traffic and user behavior, this integration helps in fine-tuning SEO strategies, developing effective content plans, and understanding the broader impact of search traffic on overall site performance.

User Section of Google Analytics 4

The "User" section in Google Analytics 4 is a critical component designed to provide in-depth insights into the characteristics and behaviors of website visitors. Understanding the "User" data is essential for businesses and website owners to tailor their content, marketing strategies, and overall user experience to meet the needs and preferences of their audience.

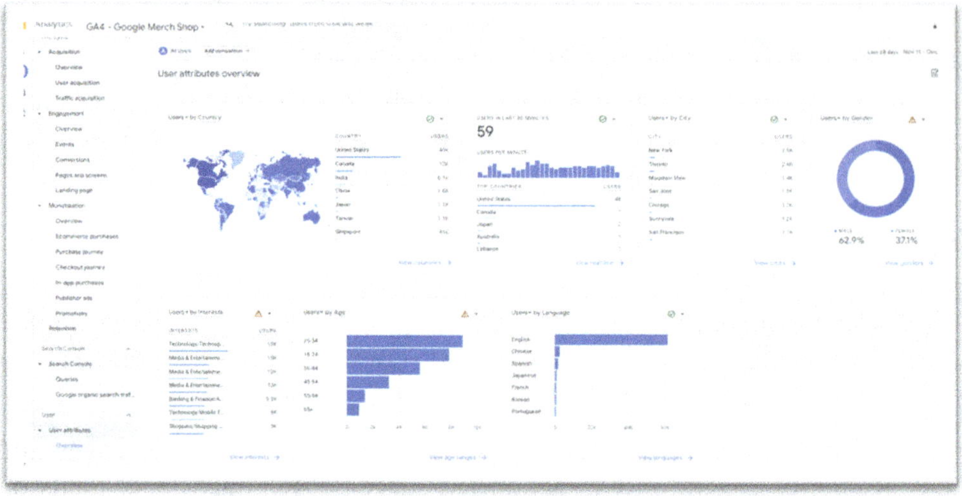

Figure 4.8 Key Features of the "User" Section

1. **User Demographics:** This feature provides data on the age, gender, and interests of your website visitors, helping you understand the composition of your audience.
2. **Geographic Information:** It shows the geographical location of users, including country, region, and city. This data is valuable for localizing content and marketing efforts.
3. **Technology Used:** This feature reports on the devices, operating systems, and browsers that visitors use to access your site, offering insights for optimizing website performance across different platforms.
4. **User Behavior:** GA4 tracks user behavior, including the frequency of visits, engagement metrics, and the user journey through your website.

Benefits of Analyzing User Data in GA4

- **Targeted Marketing:** Understanding your audience demographics helps in creating more targeted and effective marketing campaigns.
- **Content Personalization:** Insights into user preferences and interests can guide content creation, ensuring it resonates with your audience.
- **Optimized User Experience:** Knowledge of the devices and browsers used by your audience can help in optimizing the website for better user experience and performance.

Using the "User" Section for Strategic Insights

- **Audience Segmentation:** GA4 allows for the creation of custom audience segments based on user data, enabling more precise targeting in marketing efforts.
- **Cross-Device Analysis:** Understanding how users interact with your site across different devices can inform cross-platform content strategies.
- **User Retention Analysis:** The "User" section can help in analyzing how different user segments return to the site over time, informing strategies to improve user retention.

How to Access the "User" Section in GA4

To access the "User" section in GA4:

1. Log into your Google Analytics account.
2. Navigate to the appropriate GA4 property.
3. In the left sidebar, find and click on the "User" section to access reports on demographics, technology, and behavior.

The "User" section in Google Analytics 4 is a treasure trove of information about the people who visit your website. By effectively analyzing this data, businesses can gain valuable insights into who their users are, what they are interested in, and how they interact with the site. This understanding is crucial for developing user-centric strategies, optimizing the online experience, and ultimately driving growth and success in the digital landscape.

Google Analytics 4 is a powerful tool that offers enhanced capabilities to understand and analyze customer behavior across multiple platforms. For students and newcomers, starting with the basics of setting up an account, understanding the event-driven data model, and exploring the reporting interface is crucial. As you become more comfortable with the platform, delving into advanced analysis, and utilizing predictive insights can provide significant strategic value to businesses and marketers alike. With its focus on user privacy and cross-platform measurement, GA4 is well-equipped to handle the challenges of modern digital analytics.

Key Terms to know for Google Analytics 4

1. **Google Analytics 4 (GA4):** The latest version of Google Analytics, designed to provide more advanced and user-centric insights by focusing on events and user engagement.
2. **Event:** An action that a user takes on a website or app that can be tracked and measured in GA4. Events can include pageviews, clicks, video plays, form submissions, and more.
3. **Property:** A website, app, or digital asset that you want to track using Google Analytics. Each property has its own unique tracking code.
4. **Tracking Code:** A piece of code provided by GA4 that needs to be added to a website or app to collect data about user interactions and events.
5. **User:** An individual visitor to a website or app, identified by a unique combination of identifiers, including device and browser information.
6. **Session:** A period during which a user interacts with a website or app. Sessions are typically measured in 30-minute increments of inactivity.
7. **Pageview:** A type of event that tracks when a user views a specific page on a website or app.
8. **Event Tracking:** The process of tracking user interactions and actions on a website or app, such as button clicks, downloads, and video plays.
9. **Conversion:** When a user completes a desired action on a website or app, such as making a purchase, signing up for a newsletter, or filling out a contact form.
10. **Goal:** A predefined action or event that you want to track as a conversion in GA4. Goals help measure the success of specific activities on your site.
11. **User ID:** A unique identifier assigned to a user when they log in or register on a website or app. It allows for tracking users across devices and sessions.
12. **Event Parameters:** Additional data associated with an event, such as the value of a transaction, the category of a product viewed, or the source of a referral.
13. **Dimension:** A descriptive attribute or characteristic of data in GA4, such as page title, device type, traffic source, or geographic location.

14. **Metric:** A quantitative measurement of data in GA4, such as pageviews, bounce rate, conversion rate, or revenue.
15. **Segment:** A subset of your data that you can define and analyze separately, such as users from a specific location or those who completed a specific goal.
16. **Audience:** A group of users who share common characteristics or behaviors, used for targeted marketing efforts.
17. **Custom Report:** A customized report in GA4 that allows you to display specific data and metrics tailored to your analysis needs.
18. **E-commerce Tracking:** The ability to track online sales and revenue in GA4, including product details and transaction information.
19. **User Explorer:** A GA4 feature that allows you to track individual user journeys and interactions on your website or app.
20. **Data Retention:** The duration for which GA4 stores user data, which can be customized based on your data privacy and compliance requirements.

Understanding these key terms is essential for effectively using Google Analytics 4 to gather insights and make data-driven decisions about your website or app's performance and user engagement.

Choosing the right web analytics tool is a strategic decision that can significantly influence the effectiveness of a business's online strategy. Each tool offers unique strengths, making them suitable for different purposes and business sizes. Google Analytics 4 is a versatile option for a wide range of businesses, Adobe Analytics caters to enterprise-level needs, Hotjar provides excellent usability insights, and Mixpanel excels in product and user analytics. Understanding these tools and their capabilities is crucial for any business aiming to leverage web data for success in the digital landscape.

Note: further education on digital analytics will cover only aspects of Google Analytics 4 in future chapters of this book.

Key Points:

1. Web analytics tools are crucial in digital marketing and website management for tracking, analyzing, and reporting on website data.
2. Selecting the right web analytics tool is essential for obtaining relevant insights tailored to specific business needs and goals.
3. Google Analytics 4 (GA4) offers event-based tracking, cross-platform tracking, and predictive analytics, ideal for businesses seeking an integrated user interaction view.
4. Adobe Analytics provides advanced segmentation, real-time analytics, and multichannel data collection, suitable for large enterprises with deep real-time insights requirements.
5. Hotjar focuses on qualitative user behavior analysis, including heatmaps and session recordings, beneficial for UX/UI designers and website managers.
6. Mixpanel specializes in user analytics with event tracking, funnel analysis, and A/B testing, perfect for product managers and digital marketers.
7. GA4 and Adobe Analytics are leading tools, each with unique strengths: GA4 is known for its user-friendly interface and integration with Google products, while Adobe Analytics offers flexibility in data analysis and customization.
8. Understanding GA4's key changes, such as event-driven data models, cross-platform tracking, and enhanced reporting, is vital for leveraging it for strategic insights.
9. The integration of Google Search Console with GA4 provides crucial SEO optimization insights and a holistic view of traffic sources.
10. The "User" section in GA4 is essential for in-depth insights into visitor characteristics and behaviors, aiding in tailoring marketing strategies and user experiences.

Discussion Questions:

1. How do the features and capabilities of GA4 and Adobe Analytics cater to different types of businesses and their specific analytics needs?
2. In what ways can tools like Hotjar and Mixpanel complement the data obtained from more comprehensive analytics tools like GA4 or Adobe Analytics?
3. How does the event-driven data model of GA4 enhance the understanding of user behavior compared to traditional session-based tracking?
4. What are the key considerations for a business when choosing between GA4 and Adobe Analytics, considering factors like market share, integration capabilities, and customization?
5. How can integrating Google Search Console with GA4 enhance a website's SEO strategy and overall digital marketing efforts?

Chapter Five:
Digital User Experiences & Analysis

5.1 Introduction

In the dynamic field of web analytics, the ability to decipher digital consumer behavior holds the key to optimizing digital experiences and driving meaningful outcomes. Every interaction, from a click to a scroll, is a piece of the puzzle that can unlock valuable insights into your audience's preferences, challenges, and motivations. In this chapter, we embark on a journey to explore the multifaceted world of digital consumer journeys and paths through the lenses of consumer journey mapping, clickstream/pathing analysis, heatmaps, and web replays.

Our journey begins with the art of consumer journey mapping, a technique that allows us to chart the intricate course digital consumers take as they engage with your website or application. We will delve into the process of creating visual representations of these journeys, offering a holistic view of consumer pathways, touchpoints, and decision-making moments. This approach enables us to identify critical junctures in the consumer journey, helping us better understand consumer intent and areas that require optimization.

Moving forward, we will explore clickstream and pathing analysis, where we follow the digital breadcrumbs left by digital consumers as they navigate through your digital ecosystem. By meticulously examining the click-by-click progression, we can uncover behavioral patterns, track consumer flows, and pinpoint drop-off points. This insight allows us to fine-tune the consumer experience and enhance conversion rates by making data-driven adjustments.

Heatmaps are our next stop on this analytical journey. These visual representations provide a temperature gauge of consumer interactions, highlighting hotspots of activity and areas that may go unnoticed. By decoding the colors that signify clicks, scrolls, and hovers, we gain a deeper understanding of what captures consumer attention and what requires improvement.

Lastly, we delve into the world of web replays, a unique opportunity to step into the consumer's shoes and witness their experiences firsthand. By reviewing anonymized recordings of real consumer sessions, we gain unparalleled insights into their frustrations, moments of delight, and pain points. Armed with this knowledge, we can make informed decisions to optimize the consumer journey and drive engagement.

This chapter serves as your compass, guiding you through the multifaceted world of web analytics and unveiling the secrets of digital consumer journeys and paths. Together, we will uncover actionable insights that will empower you to better understand, optimize, and enhance the digital experiences of your audience. Welcome to the world of web analytics and the exploration of the digital consumer journey.

5.2 User Journey Mapping

Sponder and Gohar (2018) define the customer journey as the path taken to find and purchase products. Understanding a customer's "pain points" and guiding them through a smooth customer experience (CX) can help to generate loyal customers and advocates and improve a company's consumer lifetime value, which is a particular challenge in today's competitive environment. When a customer first discovers an item, they seldom decide to buy it right away. Customers often study a product or brand many times before making a decision (especially for certain, higher-stakes purchase decisions). The method through which a customer is made aware of a product is referred to as a touchpoint. It is through these touchpoints that the consumer journey takes place.

Customer Journey Engagement

There is a variety of media that may be used as points of engagement. Offline advertising media include television commercials, radio spots, newspaper inserts, and billboard advertisements. These types of advertising can be difficult to trace, unless outfitted with QR codes or shortened URLs to track user behavior. Blogs, manufacturer websites, website banner adverts, opinion forums, and experience portals are some of the most intriguing touchpoints for online marketing.

In offline advertising, it is difficult to map the customer journey, as it is practically impossible to say with certainty how each visitor has learned about a brand or product. Examples of offline touchpoints include recommendations from relatives or friends (word of mouth), a leaflet, or a newspaper advertisement. A qualitative survey may be able to assist in determining the medium through which engagement has taken place.

The Stages of the Customer Buying Journey

The customer journey is made up of behavioral stages a customer exhibits in the context of a digital marketing strategy. The focus of digital strategy is to influence and guide a consumer through every stage of the customer journey. Within each stage, various behavioral metrics can be evaluated to understand the impact of the advertising in question. Each stage of the customer journey maps the beginning and end points for the customer experience. This is true regardless of whether the journey is online or offline: the entire experience, from a digital strategy perspective, starts with a digital engagement; it could, nevertheless, result in a physical (offline) interaction (Singh et al., 2020). We will now look at the five stages of the customer journey in detail.

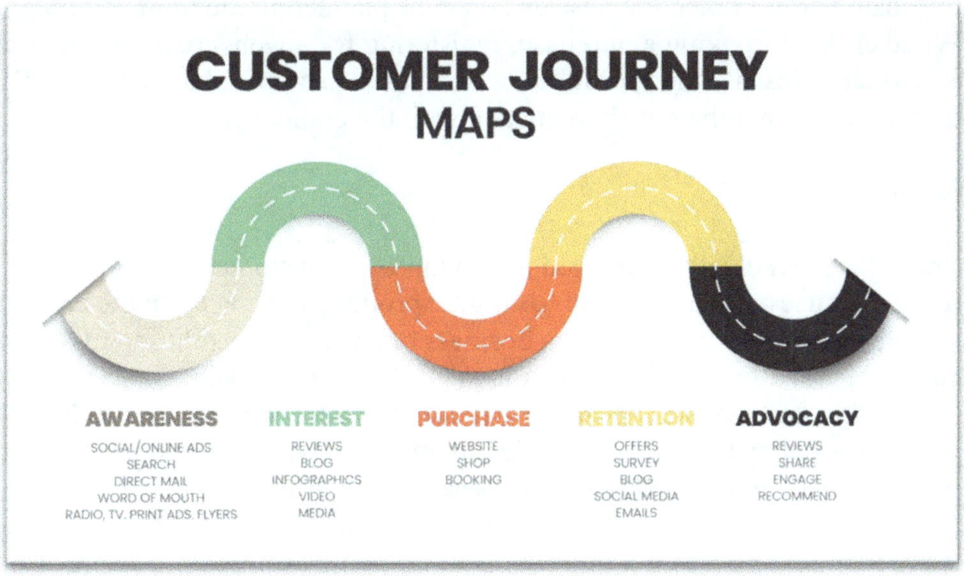

Figure 5.1 Five Stages of Customer Journey

Awareness

Through advertising (or some type of digital marketing), potential customers are exposed to or made aware of a company. After learning of a need or demand, a potential customer discovers a company through a search engine, word of mouth, a website, a testimonial, or a social media post. Although a wide net must be cast for optimal engagement with potential customers to be achieved (which can be challenging), this can be a rewarding strategy. Relevant, eye-catching, and action-driven tactics are needed to capture the attention of the customer at this stage.

Interest

After a customer has been made aware of a company through advertising, they are then exposed to an evaluation of the content or digital element. The evaluation is an overall review of the content, which allows them to deliberate on whether the content is appealing to them. Here, the customer considers whether they need or desire what the company offering. This is a critical stage in the customer journey: through this decision-making process, companies can ensure a positive marketing message and impression of the consumer experience is received by the potential customer.

Purchase

This stage involves the actual attainment of the potential customer. Here, the customer has taken the desired action as planned in the digital strategy. Whether this is making a purchase, registering for a website, or opting into a service, this is the point at which the customer has deliberately demonstrated that they wish to engage with the company.

Retention

This stage details the repeated behavior of a customer, whereby they repeatedly use or visit a company's digital product or website. In the context of digital strategy, this refers to a business or a product's ability to maintain customers for a specified period. A loyal customer is one who uses a product (or service) and tries to continue buying it over time. This is a critical stage in digital strategy because it provides an opportunity for a continuous return on investment and a loyal customer base.

Advocacy

Eventually, a customer develops a loyalty to the company and becomes an advocate for, or enthusiast of, the business. These customers help build a referral base and drive additional traffic to the organization. This generates further loyalty and builds upon the customer lifetime value, which is critical to the success and long-term sustainability of an organization.

Through understanding the customer buying journey, a digital strategist can develop unique tactics to engage with and influence the customer. The ability to do this requires an ongoing review of behavioral trends, segmentation tactics, and analysis, all of which ensure that the company finds ways to communicate and derive touchpoints in the right time and place, even as shifts in customer behavior occur.

Digital Marketing Goals Along the Customer Journey

One key goal is for the customer journey strategy to remain customer centric. This term has long been a buzzword in service-oriented organizations (most notably financial services). Customers tend to appreciate customer-centric actions taken by the company, e.g., offering one-step shopping solutions that save those customers time and money. Companies may provide a complete set of high-end services to individuals with higher incomes. It is important for the digital strategist to align the customer journey with the needs and wants of the target customer.

A basic business premise here is that giving consumers the best possible service results in loyal consumers, i.e., those who spend more time with the company and are less likely to shop around based on price. Companies choose a client-centric approach for a variety of reasons, the most notable of which is the difficulty in acquiring new clients. Some customers will compare a company to its competitors. This can be avoided if said company is selling a brand-new product or service. Acquiring new customers is frequently an expensive process that necessitates the usage of discounts or exclusive offers. As this is the case, a business may make more money by retaining its current clients.

The customer-centric approach aligns with the fundamental marketing goals of acquisition, retention, and overall interaction with a company. A company may aim to deliver an experience so unique that its customers cannot imagine receiving the same level of service and attention from another company. Naturally, a company's ability to deliver a large number of products and services while maintaining excellent quality is limited. Some client-focused firms go too far with their service offerings, compromising the key services that set them apart in the first place. In this case, overdoing customer-centric service is just as bad as not doing it at all.

Organizations that wish to go from a product-centric strategy to a customer-centric strategy must first transition from an "inside-out" to an "outside-in" mindset. The best place to start is with the customers themselves. This includes engaging with consumers, analyzing their attitudes and behaviors, and learning their expectations. Knowing which channels a customer chooses for certain demands helps to create a picture of channel usage among various customer personas and profiles.

5.3 Customer Journey Goals

Many companies seek to focus more on their customers, and the battle for the greatest customer experience is ever-intensifying. It is no longer enough to offer low prices and bombard customers with special offers. We must assume that customers are smarter than ever before, with the majority of them already knowing everything there is to know about products and services thanks to internet research. Well-informed customers anticipate a certain level of connection and service from a company.

What is ultimately critical to the success of a customer journey strategy is detailing the associated goals and using them to validate whether a strategy was a success or a failure. The first step in improving customer experience should be determining the main objectives. Customer experience is a strategic goal for improving sales and revenue. For that reason, it is necessary for a company to have a clear idea of its goals. After these goals have been identified, it is necessary to figure out how to effectively prioritize and segment them.

Some of the metrics a company may employ for forming these objectives are client retention, customer satisfaction, product purchases, purchase volume, purchase frequency, products returned, the number of disgruntled customers, and income. These metrics enable a company to evaluate how well its customer experience strategy is translating into financial results. These should be quantifiable and measurable.

The customer's perceptions—not the company's—are the focus of customer experience improvement. To improve customer experience, a picture of the consumer's ideal engagement must be created. This includes their expectations at each point of the customer life cycle, as well as interactions with the company and the challenges that may arise. There are various avenues a company can take in order to understand the consumer's perspective. This could be done by conducting surveys, holding focus groups, or running workshops. Such activities assist in mapping a larger picture of the customer journey.

5.4 Customer Journey Mapping and Omnichannel Experiences

Sponder and Khan (2018) state that "the process of generating a customer journey map (a visual tale of customers' interactions with a brand), is known as customer journey mapping or user journey mapping" (p. 206). To begin, all potential customer touchpoints are identified, such as websites, social media outlets, and contacts with marketing and sales personnel. For each buyer profile, user journeys are then constructed in relation to these numerous touchpoints. For example, a customer between the ages of 23 and 39 may first learn about a product on social media and later investigate it on the company website before making a purchase on a desktop computer. A customer journey map should incorporate the customer experience at each touchpoint. This could include what the customer needs to do and how the brand reacts. As it is a strategic tool for better understanding consumer expectations, customer journey mapping is crucial for enhancing the customer experience.

All companies, whether small, medium, or large in size, should map out their customers' journeys. Customer expectations are constantly evolving for all businesses. Regardless of a business's size, its customers expect omnichannel customer service, marketing, and sales experience. A highly personalized experience is desirable to customers, and marketing and customer service initiatives should reflect this. Omnichannel marketing and omnichannel customer service are terms used to describe this integrated strategy.

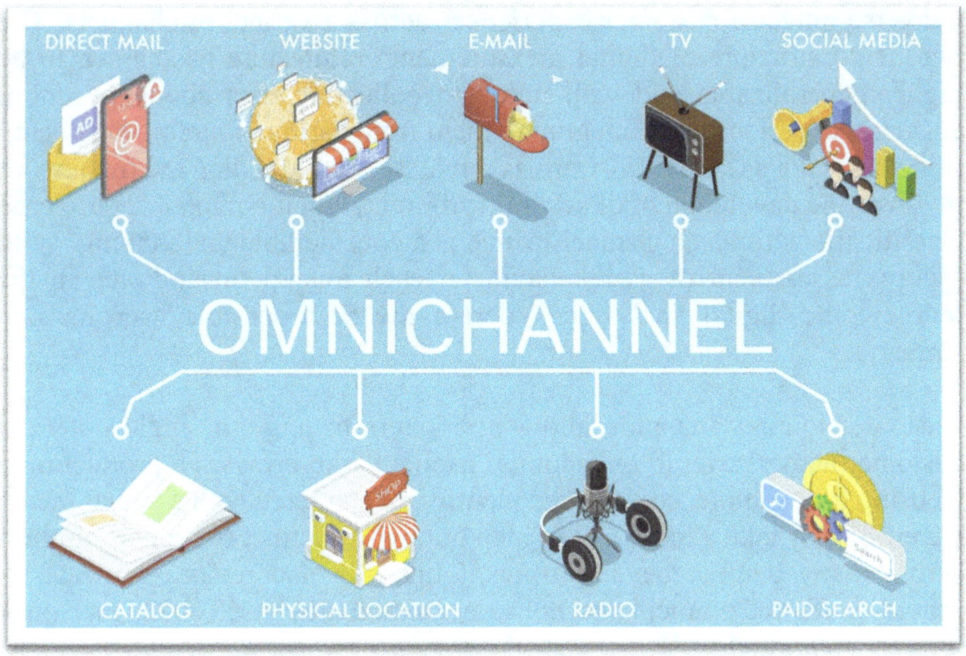

Figure 5.2 Omnichannel Marketing

Examples of omnichannel marketing include creating consistent customer experiences across channels (in terms of branding and messaging), integrating physical, digital, and mobile sales channels to support better buying experiences, and creating seamless customer journeys by ensuring that there is consistency during cross-channel engagements (Davey, 2016).

A call for organizational change is critical to the ability to align strategic objectives with new omnichannel tactics. Davey (2016) states that "part of this means breaking down departmental siloes and transitioning towards a much 'flatter' structure, and uniting departments behind common company goals" (para. 15). Working toward this focus as a company is critical, as this helps to unify all channel management. All the channels need to be aligned with respect to how their touchpoint and interaction with the customer is part of the journey-building practices of the organization. Davey (2016) also claims that "as customers are demanding a seamless experience across all brand channels, both on- and offline, businesses are struggling to move at the speed their consumers want and need" (para. 5). There is a focus here on ensuring that the entire company is operating with these fundamental principles in mind, especially when mapping

Omnichannel Marketing

Omnichannel analytics expands the scope of digital measurement to cover a diverse range of customer experiences across a variety of channels. The two-tiered structure of digital measurement architecture has shown to be highly generalizable and well-suited to collecting data about the entire customer experience and integrating them from various sources. That being said, this is not as straightforward as it may seem. Extending the framework involves the development of several (different, albeit compatible) use case classifications for each channel, which is a considerable undertaking. With focused assessment of user behavior at each touchpoint and step in the journey, the digital analyst can derive the best possible user journey strategy.

Customer journey mapping allows marketers to target a single potential customer across several touchpoints. A client who browses a product on a website, for example, could subsequently be retargeted with a social media advert. It may take a long time to map out many distinct customer journeys across many distinct buyer profiles. This will also require a means to provide a tailored omnichannel consumer experience based on the map once it has been drafted.

5.5 Clickstream and Pathing Analysis

Clickstream and pathing analysis is a critical component of web analytics that focuses on understanding how digital consumers navigate through websites and applications. It provides valuable insights into user behavior, allowing businesses to optimize the user experience and enhance conversion rates. In this section, we will define clickstream and pathing analysis, discuss what it measures, and provide the steps for conducting effective analysis. Additionally, we will illustrate these concepts with an e-commerce use case example.

> **Definition: Clickstream and pathing analysis** refers to the process of tracking and analyzing the sequence of clicks or interactions made by digital consumers as they navigate through a website or app. It involves mapping the routes users take, identifying entry and exit points, and assessing the flow of traffic between pages. This analysis helps businesses gain a deep understanding of user behavior, enabling them to make data-driven decisions for improving the user experience.

What It Measures: Clickstream and pathing analysis measures various aspects of user interactions and behaviors, including:

1. **Page Views:** The number of times each page on a website or app is visited.
2. **Entry Points:** The pages or sources through which users initially enter the site or application.
3. **Exit Points:** The pages from which users leave the site or application.
4. **Navigation Paths:** The specific routes users take when moving from one page to another.
5. **Drop-off Points:** Pages where users abandon their sessions or fail to proceed further.
6. **Conversion Paths:** Sequences of pages that lead to desired actions, such as completing a purchase or filling out a contact form.
7. **Time Spent:** The amount of time users spends on individual pages or within specific sections of the site.

Steps of Analysis: Effective clickstream and pathing analysis involves several steps:

1. **Data Collection:** Implement tracking tools, such as Google Analytics, to collect clickstream data. Ensure that each user's interactions are logged, including page views, clicks, and timestamps.

2. **Define Objectives:** Clearly outline the objectives of your analysis. Determine what specific aspects of user behavior you want to explore or improve.
3. **Segmentation:** Segment your audience to analyze different user groups separately. This can help identify unique navigation patterns for various demographics or user types.
4. **Path Visualization:** Use visualization tools to create flowcharts or diagrams that represent user paths. This allows you to visualize the most common navigation routes and drop-off points.
5. **Identify Patterns:** Analyze the data to identify common user behaviors, such as frequently visited pages, preferred routes, and points of abandonment.
6. **Optimization:** Based on your findings, make data-driven optimizations to improve the user experience. This may involve redesigning pages, streamlining navigation, or providing clearer calls to action.

E-commerce Use Case Example: Optimizing the User Journey in an Electronics Store

Objective: The objective of this e-commerce case study is to enhance the conversion rate of an online electronics store by identifying and addressing bottlenecks in the user journey. Clickstream and pathing analysis will be employed to gain insights into user behavior and guide optimization efforts.

Background: The e-commerce website in question specializes in selling a wide range of electronic products, from smartphones and laptops to home appliances and accessories. While the site attracts a substantial amount of traffic, the conversion rate—specifically, the percentage of visitors who complete a purchase—has been underperforming.

Steps:

1. **Data Collection:**
    - To initiate the analysis, the e-commerce site implements Google Analytics, a powerful tracking tool that records user interactions.
    - Key data points tracked include page views, product page visits, items added to the shopping cart, checkout steps, and timestamps of these actions.

2. **Segmentation:**
    - The user base is segmented into distinct groups based on numerous factors, including demographics (age, gender, location), device types (desktop, mobile, tablet), and referral sources (organic search, paid ads, social media).
    - This segmentation allows for a more granular analysis of different user behaviors and preferences.
3. **Path Visualization:**
    - Clickstream data is utilized to create visual representations of the user journey. Flowcharts and diagrams are generated to illustrate the paths users take from the moment they land on the website to the completion of a purchase.
    - The visualization process helps identify common routes, popular pages, and points where users tend to drop off.
4. **Identify Patterns:**
    - After comprehensive analysis, patterns and trends emerge from the clickstream and pathing data.
    - One significant observation is that a substantial number of users frequently visit product pages but abandon their shopping carts before completing a purchase.
    - Another noteworthy finding is that users arriving at the site through paid advertising campaigns have a notably higher conversion rate compared to those from organic search.
5. **Optimization:**
    - Armed with these insights, the e-commerce store begins implementing optimization strategies:
        - **Simplified Checkout Process:** Recognizing the high cart abandonment rate, the checkout process is streamlined to reduce friction. Fewer steps are required, and clearer calls to action are introduced.
        - **Increased Investment in Paid Advertising:** Given the success of paid advertising campaigns in converting users, the store allocates more resources to target potential customers effectively through online ads.
        - **Personalization:** Personalized product recommendations and tailored offers are introduced to engage users and encourage them to complete their purchases.

- **Enhanced Mobile Experience:** As mobile users represent a significant portion of the traffic, the website undergoes mobile optimization to ensure a seamless shopping experience for smartphone and tablet users.

Results: As the optimization strategies are implemented and the website's user journey is refined, the e-commerce store begins to see improvements in its conversion rate. The simplified checkout process results in fewer abandoned carts, and the increased investment in paid advertising pays off with higher conversion rates from those channels.

Over time, the website's overall conversion rate steadily increases, leading to an uptick in sales and revenue. Additionally, the improved user experience enhances customer satisfaction and loyalty, reinforcing the store's position in the highly competitive online electronics market.

In conclusion, this e-commerce use case exemplifies how clickstream and pathing analysis can be instrumental in identifying pain points in the user journey and guiding optimization efforts, ultimately resulting in a more efficient and profitable online shopping experience.

5.6 Pathing Analysis in Google Analytics 4

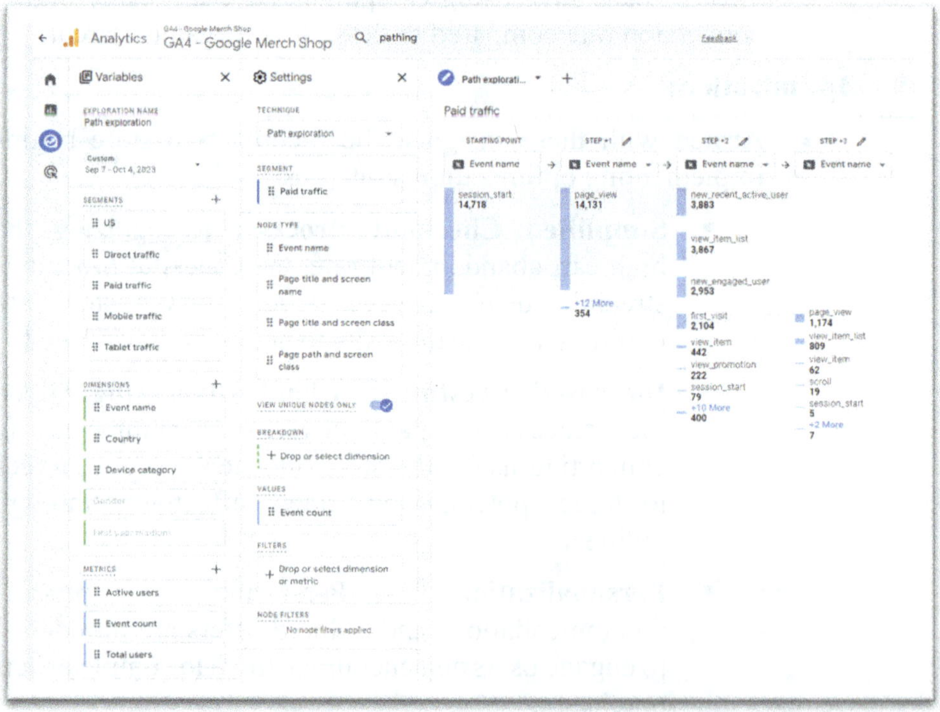

Figure 5.3 Example of Pathing Analysis in Google Analytics 4

Conducting a pathing analysis in Google Analytics 4 (GA4) using the Explore function involves several steps. Here is a guide to help you navigate through this process:

1. **Access the Explore Section**:
   - Log into your Google Analytics 4 property.
   - Navigate to the "Explore" section. This can typically be found in the menu on the left side of your GA4 interface.
2. **Create a New Exploration**:
   - In the Explore section, click on "Blank" or select a template that best suits your needs for pathing analysis. The blank option allows you to start from scratch.
3. **Choose a Technique**:
   - Select the "Path exploration" technique from the available options. This technique is specifically designed for analyzing user paths through your website or app.
4. **Define Your Population**:
   - Set up the population of users you want to analyze. This could be all users, users who completed a specific event, or users who reached a particular page.
5. **Set Up Starting and Ending Points (Optional)**:
   - You can define specific starting and ending points for the paths you want to analyze. For example, you might start with a homepage visit and end with a purchase.
6. **Configure Pathing Options**:
   - Choose the type of path you are interested in, such as user paths or event paths.
   - Specify the number of path steps you want to analyze (e.g., up to ten steps).
7. **Add Dimensions and Metrics**:
   - Add relevant dimensions (e.g., Page title or Screen class) and metrics (e.g., Event count or User count) to your exploration. This will allow you to see more detailed information about the paths users are taking.
8. **Apply Segments (Optional)**:
   - You can apply segments to your pathing analysis to narrow down your focus. For example, you might analyze paths only

for users from a specific geographic location or those using a certain type of device.

9. **Run the Exploration**:
    - Once you have configured your path exploration, click the "Run" button to generate the path analysis.

10. **Analyze the Results**:

- Examine the pathing visualization to understand how users are navigating through your site or app.
- Look for common paths, unexpected navigations, or drop-offs that might indicate areas for improvement.

11. **Adjust and Iterate**:

- Based on your findings, you might want to adjust your exploration settings or segments and rerun the analysis.
- Use the insights gained to inform changes to your website or app to improve user experience and conversion rates.

5.7 Heatmaps and Web Session Replays

Heatmaps:

What They Are: Heatmaps are graphical representations of data that visually display the intensity or concentration of user interactions on a web page. They use color coding to highlight areas where users click, move their mouse, or spend the most time. There are three primary types of heatmaps:

1. **Click Heatmaps:** Show where users click on a webpage, helping to identify popular links and elements.
2. **Move Heatmaps:** Indicate where users move their mouse cursor, giving insights into areas of interest or confusion.
3. **Scroll Heatmaps:** Illustrate how far users scroll down a webpage, revealing content engagement and drop-off points.

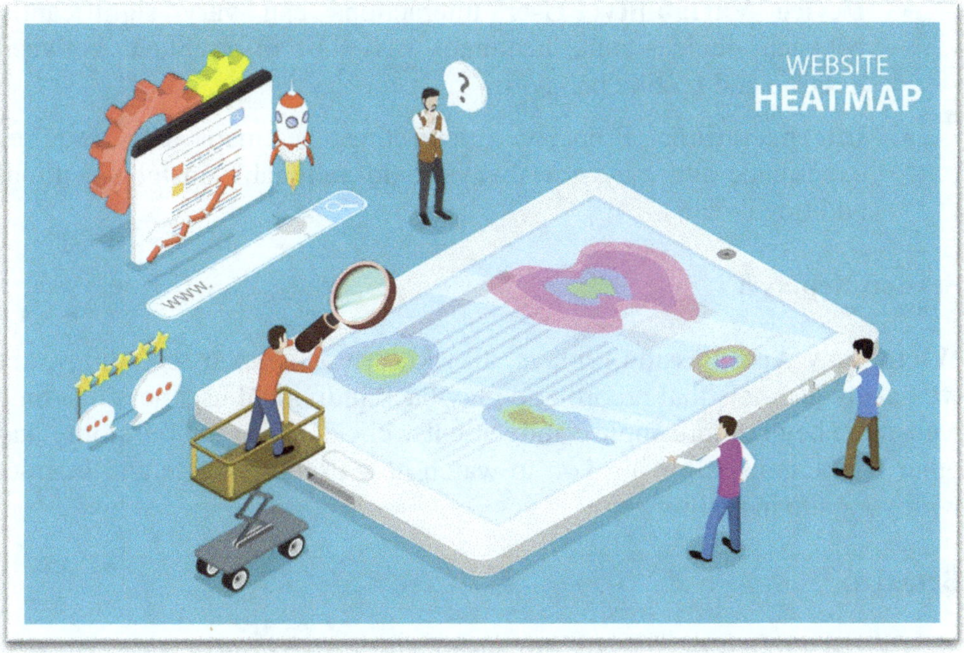

Figure 5.4 Heatmap on Website Example

The above figure is an example of what a heatmap for a website may look like. This heatmap shows varying colors over a webpage layout, indicating areas of high and low user interaction, with bright colors like red and orange for high interaction zones and cooler colors like blue and green for less interacted areas.

Heatmap Benefits:

- **Visual Insights:** Heatmaps provide a quick and easy-to-understand visual representation of user behavior, making it simple to identify patterns.
- **Optimization:** They help website owners optimize page layouts, calls-to-action, and content placement by highlighting areas of high and low user engagement.
- **A/B Testing:** Heatmaps can be used in conjunction with A/B testing to assess the impact of design changes or new features.

Heatmap Challenges:

- **Limited Context:** Heatmaps may not provide the full context of user behavior, such as why users click or do not click on certain elements.

- **Device Variability:** User interactions can vary significantly between devices, and heatmaps may not differentiate between desktop and mobile behavior.
- **Interpretation:** Properly interpreting heatmap data requires experience and may not always yield actionable insights without additional data.

Session Replays:

What They Are: Session replays, also known as session recordings, are web analytics tools that record and play back individual user sessions on a website. They capture mouse movements, clicks, form submissions, and other interactions, allowing you to watch how users navigate and interact with your site in real time.

Benefits:

- **User Behavior Analysis:** Session replays offer an in-depth view of user behavior, helping you understand how visitors experience your website.
- **Bug Identification:** They can be invaluable in identifying technical issues, such as broken links, form submission errors, or usability problems.
- **User Testing:** Session replays can be used for user testing and usability studies, providing valuable feedback on user experiences.

Challenges:

- **Privacy Concerns:** Recording and replaying user sessions can raise privacy and compliance concerns, especially in regions with strict data protection regulations.
- **Data Volume:** Session replay data can be vast, making it challenging to process and analyze effectively.
- **Resource Intensive:** The technology required to capture and replay sessions can be resource-intensive, potentially impacting website performance.
- **Selective Insights:** While session replays provide detailed information on individual sessions, they may not always reveal broader trends or patterns in user behavior.

In summary, heatmaps and session replays are valuable tools in web analytics, providing insights into user behavior and website performance. They offer unique benefits in terms of visualization and in-depth analysis but also come with challenges related to privacy, data volume, and interpretation. Web analysts often use a combination of these tools, along with other analytics methods, to gain a comprehensive understanding of user interactions and optimize their websites for better user experiences.

In conclusion, this chapter has underscored the critical significance of analyzing digital consumer journey behavior in today's ever-evolving business landscape. In an era where online interactions have become a primary avenue for customer engagement, understanding how users navigate digital spaces is paramount for organizations seeking to thrive and succeed.

We began by delving into the concept of pathing analysis, which provided valuable insights into the sequences of steps users take when interacting with digital platforms. This method not only illuminated the common routes users follow but also identified bottlenecks and opportunities for optimization. It allowed businesses to make data-driven decisions, streamline user experiences, and enhance conversion rates.

Furthermore, our exploration of customer journeys demonstrated the holistic nature of user interactions. By mapping out the entire lifecycle of a customer's experience, we gained a deeper understanding of their needs, pain points, and motivations. This insight empowered businesses to tailor their strategies, content, and offerings to meet user expectations at each stage of their journey, ultimately fostering customer loyalty and satisfaction.

Heatmaps emerged as a powerful tool for visualizing user engagement and attention. By providing a spatial representation of where users click, hover, or scroll, heatmaps enabled businesses to identify the areas of their digital assets that garnered the most attention. Armed with this knowledge, organizations could make informed decisions about content placement, call-to-action buttons, and design improvements to optimize user engagement.

Session replays, the final concept discussed in this chapter, brought the digital consumer journey to life. They allowed businesses to witness firsthand how users interacted with their platforms, providing an invaluable perspective on user behavior, frustrations, and successes. By dissecting session replays, organizations were able to identify pain points and usability issues, leading to targeted improvements that enhanced user satisfaction and conversion rates.

In summary, the integration of pathing analysis, customer journeys, heatmaps, and session replays into the analysis of digital consumer journey behavior equips businesses with powerful tools to navigate the complex digital landscape. These insights enable organizations to make data-driven decisions, create personalized experiences, and continually refine their digital strategies. As we move forward in an increasingly digital world, mastering the art of understanding and optimizing the digital consumer journey will be pivotal in achieving long-term success and staying ahead of the competition.

Key Points:

1. Deciphering digital consumer behavior through web analytics is crucial for optimizing digital experiences and driving meaningful outcomes.
2. Consumer journey mapping is a valuable tool for understanding the intricate paths digital consumers take, highlighting critical touchpoints and decision-making moments.
3. Clickstream/pathing analysis provides deep insights into user navigation patterns and behaviors, helping identify drop-off points and optimize user experience.
4. Heatmaps offer visual representations of user interactions on a website, indicating areas of high activity and guiding improvements in web design and content placement.
5. Web session replays allow businesses to step into their consumers' shoes, offering direct insights into user experiences, frustrations, and preferences.
6. Customer journey mapping helps in creating visual narratives of customer interactions, enhancing understanding of consumer intent and areas needing optimization.
7. Pathing analysis in tools like Google Analytics 4 is essential for tracking user pathways and understanding behavior flows within digital platforms.
8. Heatmaps and web session replays are powerful tools for a qualitative understanding of user behavior, complementing the quantitative data from traditional analytics.
9. Implementing a customer-centric approach in digital marketing involves focusing on the customer's perspectives and tailoring strategies accordingly.
10. Omnichannel analytics and customer journey mapping are critical for providing a seamless, integrated consumer experience across various digital touchpoints.

Discussion Questions:

1. How can businesses effectively use consumer journey mapping to enhance customer experience and identify areas for improvement in their digital strategy?
2. What are the advantages of combining quantitative methods like clickstream analysis with qualitative tools like heatmaps and session replays in web analytics?
3. How can pathing analysis in tools like Google Analytics 4 be utilized to optimize user pathways and improve overall website effectiveness?
4. In what ways can a customer-centric approach and omnichannel experiences be integrated into a company's digital marketing strategy to enhance customer engagement?
5. How can heatmaps and session replays provide deeper insights into user behavior, and what are their implications for website design and content strategy?

Chapter Six: Search Analytics

6.1 Introduction

In the ever-evolving digital landscape, the ability to harness the potential of search engines has become a defining factor for online success. Whether you are a business aiming to expand your digital footprint or a marketer seeking to understand customer behavior, the world of web analytics holds a treasure trove of insights waiting to be unearthed. Central to this endeavor is the realm of Search Analytics, a dynamic field that interlaces the twin pillars of Search Engine Optimization (SEO) and Search Engine Marketing (SEM). In this chapter, we embark on a journey into the fascinating universe of Search Analytics, where data-driven decision-making meets the art of enhancing online visibility.

Understanding SEO and SEM

Before delving into the intricacies of Search Analytics, it is essential to grasp the foundational concepts of SEO and SEM:

Search Engine Optimization (SEO): SEO is the craft of fine-tuning your digital presence to organically rank higher on search engine results pages (SERPs). It is a multifaceted approach that encompasses everything from keyword research and on-page optimization to technical enhancements and content strategy. In essence, SEO aims to make your website more appealing to search engines, subsequently increasing its visibility to users searching for related information, products, or services. It is a long-term strategy with the potential for substantial, sustainable results.

Search Engine Marketing (SEM): On the other hand, SEM is a broader category that includes both paid and organic tactics to increase a website's visibility on search engines. While SEO falls under the organic (unpaid) umbrella, SEM incorporates paid advertising, commonly referred to as Pay-Per-Click (PPC) advertising. SEM allows businesses to bid on keywords and display ads in the sponsored sections of search engine results. It offers immediate visibility, making it an effective strategy for driving targeted traffic, especially when complementing an SEO campaign.

The Role of Search Analytics

Search Analytics serves as the nexus where SEO and SEM converge, offering a panoramic view of the performance, impact, and potential for improvement within the realm of search engine visibility. It is the compass that guides digital marketers, businesses, and website owners in navigating the intricate maze of search engine algorithms and user intent. Here is a glimpse of what you can expect to discover in this chapter:

1. **Unpacking the SEO Toolbox:** We will delve into the world of SEO analytics, exploring how tools and metrics can illuminate the effectiveness of your SEO efforts. From keyword tracking and backlink analysis to website audits and rank monitoring, you will gain insights into the arsenal at your disposal for optimizing your digital presence.
2. **SEM Metrics that Matter:** Understanding the performance of your SEM campaigns is crucial in managing your digital advertising budget effectively. We will demystify SEM metrics, from Click-Through Rates (CTR) and Quality Scores to Cost-Per-Click (CPC) and Conversion Rates. These insights will enable you to refine your SEM strategies and maximize the ROI on your paid advertising campaigns.
3. **Integrating SEO and SEM:** The synergy between SEO and SEM is where the magic happens. You will discover how these two disciplines can complement each other to create a harmonious digital marketing strategy. By aligning your organic and paid efforts, you can amplify your online presence, achieve greater visibility, and ultimately drive more qualified traffic to your website.
4. **Leveraging Data-Driven Decisions:** Data is the lifeblood of Search Analytics. We will explore how to collect, analyze, and interpret data to make informed decisions that steer your SEO and SEM initiatives in the right direction. From uncovering keyword opportunities to fine-tuning ad campaigns, you will learn how to harness the power of data to achieve your online goals.

As we venture deeper into the world of Search Analytics, you will come to appreciate how these insights can revolutionize your digital strategy. Whether you are aiming to climb the organic rankings, optimize your paid advertising efforts, or strike the perfect balance between the two, Search Analytics is the compass that will guide you on your quest for digital supremacy. So, fasten your seatbelts and get ready to embark on an exciting journey through the labyrinth of search engines and the captivating realm of web analytics.

6.2 Keyword Research and Analysis

Keywords are the cornerstones of digital marketing strategies, particularly in the realms of Search Engine Optimization (SEO) and Search Engine Marketing (SEM). A profound understanding of keyword research and analysis is pivotal for businesses and marketers seeking to enhance their online visibility and effectively target their audiences. In this chapter, we will embark on an extensive journey into the world of keyword research and analysis, diving deep into how it intertwines with web analytics and forms the backbone of successful SEO and SEM campaigns.

Understanding Keyword Research

The Significance of Keywords:

Keywords serve as the digital breadcrumbs that guide users to discover websites and content. These are the words or phrases individuals type into search engines when seeking information, products, or services. Keyword research involves uncovering the precise words and phrases users are likely to employ to find your website or offerings.

User Intent:

Effective keyword research goes beyond identifying popular words; it hinges on comprehending user intent. Users employ different search queries based on their intent—whether it is to gain information, locate a specific webpage, or make a purchase. Successful keyword research seeks to align content and offerings with user intentions.

Tools and Resources:

- **Keyword Research Tools:** Utilizing tools such as Google Keyword Planner, SEMrush, and Ahrefs is indispensable for identifying relevant keywords, assessing their search volume, gauging competition, and tracking trends.
- **Competitor Analysis:** Examining competitors' websites provides valuable insights into keywords they are ranking for, helping uncover opportunities and refine your strategy.
- **Customer Feedback:** Customer reviews, feedback, and inquiries can yield insights into the language your target audience uses when conducting online searches.

6.3 The Role of Keyword Research in SEO

On-Page Optimization:

Keyword research lays the foundation for on-page SEO efforts. It guides the strategic placement of keywords in critical areas such as page titles, headings, meta descriptions, and content, making webpages more appealing to search engine algorithms.

Content Creation:

Keyword research steers content creation endeavors. By identifying target keywords, you can craft high-quality, informative content that addresses users' queries and ranks prominently on search engine results pages (SERPs).

Long-Tail Keywords:

Long-tail keywords, which are specific, often lengthier keyword phrases, have the potential to attract highly targeted traffic. Effective keyword research unveils these valuable gems, which may have lower competition and yield higher conversion rates.

Monitoring and Adaptation:

Keyword research is an ongoing endeavor. Regularly revisiting and updating your keyword strategy is vital to stay attuned to evolving search trends and shifting user behaviors.

Keyword Research and SEM

Paid Search Advertising:

In SEM, keyword research is fundamental to paid search advertising. It entails the selection of keywords for which you want your ads to appear. Advertisers bid on these keywords, and their ads are displayed when users search for those specific terms.

Quality Score:

Your choice of keywords directly affects your Quality Score in platforms like Google Ads. A higher Quality Score can lower your ad costs and enhance ad placement, making keyword research pivotal for cost-effective SEM campaigns.

Negative Keywords:

Identifying negative keywords, which are irrelevant or undesired search terms, is imperative to optimize your ad spend and ensure your ads are shown to the most relevant audience.

Integrating Keyword Research with Web Analytics

Google Analytics and Search Console:

Google Analytics and Google Search Console offer invaluable insights into keyword performance. These tools provide data on organic traffic, keyword rankings, click-through rates, and conversion rates. This data empowers you to track the effectiveness of your keyword strategy.

User Behavior Analysis:

Web analytics tools enable you to scrutinize user behavior on your website. You can ascertain which keywords are driving traffic, assess how long users stay on your site, and evaluate whether they are converting. These insights aid in refining your keyword strategy and optimizing landing pages.

A/B Testing:

A/B testing entails creating two versions of a webpage—one with different keywords—and measuring which performs better in terms of user engagement and conversions. Web analytics tools furnish the requisite data for conducting these tests effectively.

Advanced Keyword Analysis Techniques

- **Semantic Keywords:** Beyond exact-match keywords, semantic keywords—words and phrases related to your primary keywords—are critical for crafting comprehensive, authoritative content that meets user intent.

Example 1: Content Relevance and User Intent

Suppose you have a website selling hiking gear, and your primary keyword is "hiking boots." Analyzing semantic keywords related to "hiking boots," such as "waterproof hiking boots," "summer hiking boots," or "best hiking boot brands," can help you create more relevant and comprehensive content. This content addresses various aspects of the user's intent, whether they are looking for specific features, seasonal suitability, or brand recommendations.

Example 2: Voice Search Optimization

With the rise of voice-activated assistants like Siri and Alexa, understanding semantic keywords is essential. Users often phrase voice searches in a conversational manner. For instance, someone might ask, "What are the most comfortable hiking boots for long hikes?" Recognizing and incorporating such semantic keywords into your content can improve its visibility in voice search results.

Keyword Difficulty: Analyzing keyword difficulty allows you to gauge the competitiveness of keywords and prioritize those that align with your website's authority and available resources.

Example 1: Long-Term vs. Short-Term Strategy

Let us say you operate a new e-commerce website specializing in tech gadgets. You want to target the keyword "best smartphones." However, keyword analysis reveals that this keyword has high competition and difficulty. Instead of solely pursuing this competitive term, you might decide to adopt a long-term strategy and focus on less competitive keywords, such as "best budget smartphones under $300." Over time, you can build authority and gradually target more competitive keywords.

Example 2: Resource Allocation and ROI

Keyword difficulty analysis helps you allocate your resources effectively. If you are running a pay-per-click (PPC) campaign, choosing keywords with less difficulty can result in lower advertising costs while still attracting relevant traffic. For instance, if you are a travel agency, targeting "affordable summer vacations" instead of "luxury summer travel" could provide a better return on investment, considering your budget constraints.

Seasonal Keywords: Certain keywords experience seasonal fluctuations in search volume. Recognizing and capitalizing on these trends can amplify traffic and sales during peak periods.

Example 1: Holiday and Event-Related Keywords

If you operate an online gift shop, you will want to pay attention to seasonal trends like Christmas, Valentine's Day, or Mother's Day. Analyzing seasonal keywords such as "unique Valentine's Day gifts" or "Christmas gift ideas" allows you to optimize your content and marketing efforts for these periods. By doing so, you can attract more visitors and boost sales during the holiday season.

Example 2: Weather-Dependent Keywords

For businesses related to outdoor activities or products, understanding weather-dependent keywords is crucial. For instance, if you sell swimming pool equipment, you will want to target keywords like "pool maintenance tips for summer" when warmer weather approaches and people start opening their pools. Recognizing these seasonal shifts in search volume allows you to adjust your content strategy accordingly and maximize your visibility during peak periods.

Incorporating semantic keywords, analyzing keyword difficulty, and recognizing seasonal keyword trends are advanced SEO techniques that can elevate your digital marketing strategy. They help you create content that resonates with user intent, allocate resources efficiently, and capitalize on seasonal fluctuations to drive more targeted traffic and achieve your business goals.

Conclusion: Leveraging Keyword Insights

Keyword research and analysis stand as the linchpins of SEO and SEM. They serve as the guiding compass that ensures your content and advertising strategies align with user intent. By seamlessly integrating keyword research with web analytics, you can perpetually refine your approach, stay competitive, and attract targeted traffic that converts. In the dynamic landscape of digital marketing, fluency in the language of your audience is the key to success, and keyword research equips you with the linguistic toolkit to thrive.

6.4 SEM & Paid Search Analysis

Customers often use search engines to find what they are looking for online. Paying for ad placement or keyword searches on these search engines is one key strategy in this field. This ability to grab the customer's attention almost immediately can give the company a competitive edge. These companies can employ further analysis methods to develop best practices and optimize this strategy.

Search engine marketing is the critical online competitive strategy that drives a company's momentum (and, in turn, their relevance in the marketplace). Essentially, a company must understand how it scores when compared with its competition. Search engine marketing (SEM) sees a company paying search engines (e.g., Google or Bing) for digital real estate. For example, a company can pay for elevated rankings on search results (based on specific, unique keywords). Search engines generate a substantial portion of all website traffic (Chaffey, 2020). For this reason, effective measurement and oversight of SEM strategies is crucial for reaching prospective customers.

Many online users discover companies based on their searches. Search engine optimization (SEO) is a somewhat organic process: it sees a specific search evolve over time as users input various terms or phrases. Eventually, top companies will start to appear in those results. SEO results are natural and based on a hierarchy of certain criteria (e.g., keyword relevance), and they are not manipulated by a company. In other words, a company cannot pay to influence the results (Sheffield, 2020). SEM, by comparison, is a method by which companies inorganically reach the top of the search results. In other words, they set aside an advertising budget to pay the search engine. It should be noted that companies on both ends of this divide are all competing regardless of their methods.

Paid display (i.e., banner ads) has been on the decline due to a number of factors. Most importantly, it has been replaced by more persuasive media (e.g., video ads). Add to this the problem of customer banner blindness, and we see a substantial drop in the effectiveness of paid display. Banner blindness occurs for one very obvious reason: the digital world is completely saturated with all kinds of banner advertising modules. Consumers have become desensitized to the number of shown advertisement units on websites that they can easily tune them out (or even block them entirely). Much of the time, banners are little more than background noise.

6.5 SEM Process

Keyword bidding refers to the market and technological procedures and labor required for bidding on paid search terms and managing them to maximize success. One aspect of the corresponding analysis is keyword testing, which examines the keywords and phrases most likely to be used by consumers looking for certain e-commerce platforms (and their products). Advertising, as well as any creative text therein, is shown through search engines. The content of the advertisement is, notably, limited. Above all, SEM allows a company to select the advert's score (up to the cap or their own budget) and facilitates accurate term targeting (i.e., to specific computers, browsers, and geographical locations).

Adviso (2009) provides the overview of the bidding process: The higher the rank value, the better the ad's position on the search pages. The search engine then determines how much the company pays for a click in that auction. That price depends on three factors:

1. The company's ranking among the auction competitors
2. The performance of the competitor(s) ranked below
3. The quality score

What the company pays can be calculated as follows:

$$\frac{(\text{Bid of advertiser}) \cdot \text{Quality score of advertiser}}{\text{Our quality score}} + \$0.01$$

Note that we could simplify the equation using the aforementioned rank value variable:

$$\frac{(\text{Rank value of advertiser})}{\text{Our quality score}} + \$0.01$$

This equation reveals two important pieces of information:

1. The higher the quality score, the lower the click's price.
2. The next advertiser's performance has an important influence on the click's price.

Most search advertisers use web analytics reporting to gather a large amount of first-party data from their websites to execute profitable paid search campaigns. Paying search advertisers often produce and test a vast number of keyword combinations, i.e., they have a long list of keywords to test on a daily basis. Typically, this is full-time work. Paid search advertisement includes image-rich content, and text ads are considered the most popular form of paid search ad. Text advertisements require the advertiser to define tags, summary lines, and URL. A/B checking removes the guesswork in designing good text adverts or paid search landing pages (Craig, n.d.).

Paid search impressions are defined by the possibility of seeing the advert. The bidding technique and the individual content of the text advertisement determine the cost per click (CPC) and average location. The click-through rate (CTR) is calculated by dividing the number of times an advertisement is viewed by the number of times it is pressed (Sponder & Khan, 2018).

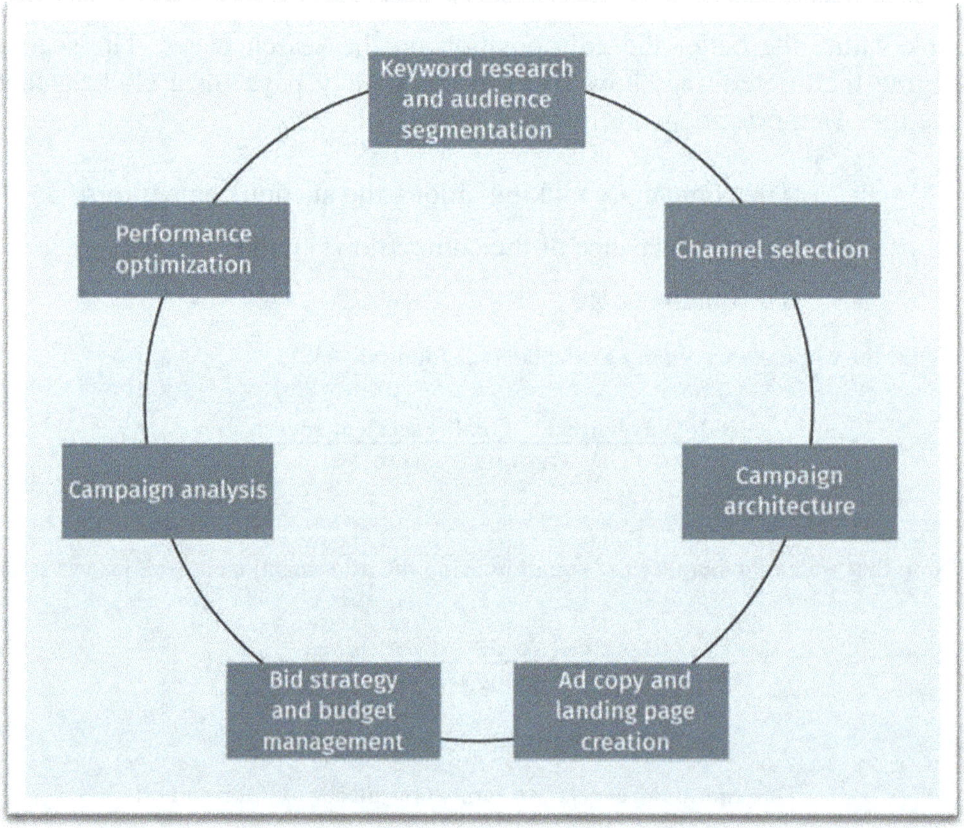

Figure 6.1 Paid Search Process and Strategy Chart

Paid search metrics can now be imported into a web analytics framework or stored inside the campaign platform (e.g., Google AdWords or Bing Advertising). In some markets, paid text advertisements are more successful than others. No component of this advertising funding has a fixed price, and the cost of the keywords used in the copy is determined by supply and demand. To determine whether the campaigns are profitable, it may be more instructive to consider the number of online users shopping in each market, as well as the importance of what is on offer. Ultimately, the focus here is on paid search funding, i.e., making a financial investment to generate the best return (ROI) possible (Craig, n.d.).

SEM KPI's

If we employ consulting resources (or do it ourselves), then our SEM campaign must be accountable in order to be effective. Depending on the priorities, the SEM key performance indicators (KPIs) can differ greatly. We will now take a closer look at some of the top KPIs in this field. First, we have the pay per click (PPC). With this online marketing technique, advertisers pay a fee each time one of their ads is clicked. Essentially, this is a way to buy website traffic rather than trying to "earn" it organically. Search engine advertising is one of the most prevalent types of PPC. Someone searching for a keyword relevant to their product will aid advertisers in paying for placement on a search engine's results page.

Next, we have the CPC, i.e., the price paid per click. A cost per thousand (CPM) is an alternative that measures the number of views (or viewers) in thousands regardless of whether each audience clicks on the commercial. CPC is particularly helpful for advertisers with a fixed budget. The advertisement is excluded from rotation for the rest of the billing cycle until the budget is met. For example, a website with a ten-cent CPC and 1,000 click-throughs will be charged a total of $100 ($0.10 · 1,000).

The quality score (QS) is a metric used by Google to determine how important a keyword is based on data from previous ad auctions. Keywords in an advertiser's account are given a QS number (up to 10) once Google has collected enough information. This scale helps marketers assess how well they are performing (concerning keyword selection), writing effective advertisements, and directing consumers to useful landing pages.

That being said, it is the real-time QS that counts. Since Google relies on advertisement sales, it has a strong desire to ensure that people find the advertisements compelling enough to engage with them. After all, Google's ad auction is built on a CPC model. In other words, it only makes money when customers interact with the advertisement (Google Ads, n.d.).

Next, we have impressions, i.e., how often the outcome or paying advertisement appears in searches. This important metric indicates how many users are seeing and clicking on the entry. An extremely negative ratio indicates two things: the SEO is in good shape, and the anchor text is failing to attract visitors (Bishop, 2021).

The percentage of branded keywords is reflected in long-tail search words that are specific to a website or company. Long-tail search words have lower search volumes and are more specific than keywords commonly inputted into search engines. They tend to be more precise, meaning a user can find a specific set of content. An increase in long-term keywords may indicate that a brand is becoming more popular (and perhaps preferred). These keywords are not necessarily a feature of online SEO. Rather, they may be a consequence of it. They indicate that the SEM strategy is producing long-term returns (Sickler, 2019).

Finally, we have the return on investment (ROI) and keyword traffic. ROI is the metric that an organization would most likely push for—particularly concerning PPC campaigns. We must remember that an organization investing money in a project expects to see a return. Patience is crucial here, as a few years could pass before the SEM provides a measurable financial benefit (Bishop, 2021). Keyword traffic is the volume traffic created by any of the keywords the company wishes to analyze or eventually use in a PPC campaign. This KPI is crucial for determining whether the SEM campaign's basics are suitable (Net Age, 2012).

Conclusion

SEM analytics measures the effectiveness of the real estate being used to track the clicks and user engagement from the paid search and displays. The page search is used to optimize the number of clicks and overall website padding. This helps a company determine whether people are converting from those search terms. This approach ensures that the keywords are evaluated and analyzed to see which keywords drive relevancy, engagement, and user action and behavior.

A dashboard should be set up to rank what is funneling the best clicks and ultimately causing conversion. For example, let us say that a company has paid for a keyword (acting as one KPI). If the clicks on the keyword fail to result in a high conversion rate, then it should be re-evaluated. Often, companies set aside a budget for SEM, and analyzing the KPIs and bidding on suboptimal keywords can impact that budget. Advertising funds must be used for bidding on the right keywords. Continuous measurement of keyword performance ensures that the right words associated with the website generate the overall conversion rate desired. Should the correct keywords have been bid upon, the company could analyze user behavior on the landing page to which the search term has brought them.

6.6 Search Queries in Google Analytics 4

The queries function in Google Analytics, sourced from Google Search Console data, provides detailed information about how users find their website through Google search.

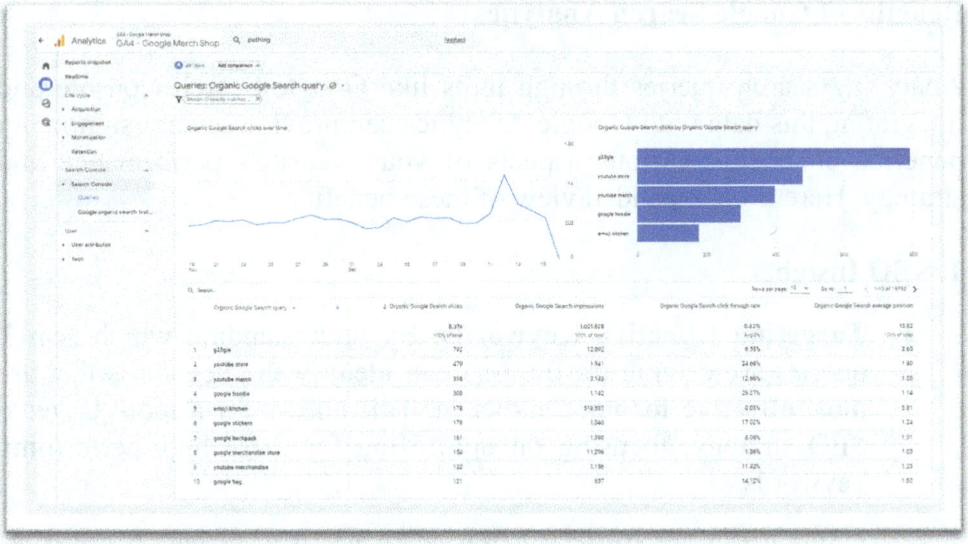

Figure 6.2 Google Analytics 4 Search Console

How it Works

1. **Data Collection**: Google Search Console tracks various metrics related to the searches that lead to your site, such as the specific search queries, the number of times your site appears in search results (impressions), the number of clicks your site receives, and the average click-through rate (CTR).

2. **Integration and Access**: Once you link your Google Search Console account with Google Analytics, this data is accessible directly within the GA interface, usually under the 'Acquisition' section.

3. **Analysis and Reporting**: In GA, you can analyze search queries data to understand which keywords are most effective in driving traffic to your site. This includes:

    - **Search Query Breakdown**: Viewing the specific queries that lead users to your site.

    - **Performance Metrics**: Analyzing clicks, impressions, CTR, and the average position of your site in search results for each query.

    - **Trend Analysis**: Observing how these metrics change over time, helping to identify trends, opportunities, and areas for improvement.

Benefits of Google Search Analytics

Analyzing search queries through tools like Google Search Console and integrating this data with Google Analytics can provide several significant benefits, enhancing various aspects of your website's performance and strategy. Here is an expanded view of these benefits:

1. SEO Insights

- **Targeting Effective Keywords**: By understanding which search queries are driving traffic, you can identify the keywords that are most effective for your audience. This allows for a more targeted SEO strategy, focusing on optimizing for these high-performing keywords.

- **Competitive Analysis**: Analyzing search queries can also provide insights into your competitors' strategies, revealing the keywords they might be targeting. This information can be used to refine your SEO tactics to compete more effectively.

- **Long-Tail Keyword Opportunities**: Search queries often reveal long-tail keywords – more specific, less common queries – that may have lower competition and higher conversion rates. Targeting these can be a highly effective SEO strategy.

2. Content Optimization

- **Enhancing Underperforming Content**: By identifying the queries that are not performing well, you can pinpoint the content that needs to be improved. This might involve refining the content, improving its relevance to specific queries, or enhancing its overall quality.

- **Meta Tag Optimization**: Search queries can guide the optimization of meta titles and descriptions, making them more relevant to the most common searches. This can increase CTR from search engine results pages (SERPs).

- **Aligning with User Search Intent**: Understanding the intent behind search queries (informational, transactional, navigational) allows you to align your content more closely with what users are seeking, potentially increasing the engagement and satisfaction of your visitors.

3. Market Understanding

- **Insight into User Behavior and Needs**: Analyzing search queries can reveal a lot about what your audience is looking for, their interests, pain points, and needs. This knowledge can drive not only content creation but also broader marketing and product development strategies.
- **Trend Identification**: Search query analysis can help in identifying emerging trends in your industry or market. By staying ahead of these trends, you can position your content and offerings to meet evolving market demands.
- **Localization and Segmentation**: Search queries can vary significantly by region and demographic. Analyzing these differences allows for more effective localization of your content and can help in segmenting your market for more targeted marketing efforts.

4. Enhanced User Experience

- **Content Personalization**: By understanding the common queries, you can personalize the content and user experience on your site to better match user expectations.
- **Navigation Improvements**: Insights from search queries can also inform website navigation and structure, making it easier for users to find the information they are looking for.

The benefits of analyzing search queries extend far beyond basic SEO. They encompass a comprehensive understanding of your audience, market trends, and content effectiveness. This analysis can inform a wide range of strategic decisions, from content creation and optimization to broader marketing and business strategies, ultimately contributing to a more successful and user-focused online presence.

Key Points:

1. Keyword research is crucial for both SEO and SEM, as it influences on-page optimization, content creation, and the effectiveness of paid search advertising.
2. Through keyword research, specific keywords are strategically placed in titles, headings, and content to make webpages more search engine friendly.
3. Target keywords guide the development of relevant and informative content, crucial for ranking on SERPs.
4. Identifying long-tail keywords can attract targeted traffic with potentially higher conversion rates due to lower competition.
5. Continuously updating and refining keyword strategies is essential to adapt to changing search trends and user behaviors.
6. In SEM, selecting the right keywords is fundamental for creating effective ad campaigns and improving Quality Scores, which can lower ad costs and enhance ad placement.
7. Tools like Google Analytics and Search Console provide insights into keyword performance and user behavior, essential for refining SEO and SEM strategies.
8. Incorporating semantic keywords, assessing keyword difficulty, and recognizing seasonal keyword trends are advanced techniques that can enhance a digital marketing strategy.
9. The SEM process involves keyword bidding, analysis, and optimization to manage paid search terms effectively, and understanding the auction process, quality score, and performance of competitors is vital for successful SEM campaigns.
10. Important SEM KPIs include PPC, CPC, quality score, impressions, percentage of branded keywords, ROI, and keyword traffic, which help assess the effectiveness of SEM campaigns.
11. GA4's integration with Google Search Console provides valuable insights into search queries leading to a site, helping in SEO optimization, content strategy, and understanding market trends.
12. Analyzing search queries offers a comprehensive understanding of audience needs, trends, and content effectiveness, which can inform strategic decisions across marketing and business operations.

Discussion Questions:

1. How can businesses effectively balance keyword research for both SEO and SEM to ensure a cohesive and effective online marketing strategy?
2. What are the key considerations for businesses when integrating keyword research with web analytics to optimize their digital marketing efforts?
3. How can understanding search queries and user behavior through tools like Google Analytics 4 enhance a company's SEO and content strategy?
4. What role do advanced keyword analysis techniques play in crafting a competitive digital marketing strategy in today's market?
5. How can businesses use the insights gained from SEM KPIs and search queries analysis to improve user experience and engagement on their websites?

Chapter Seven: Online Customer Segmentation & Analysis

7.1 Introduction

In today's digital landscape, where consumer preferences shift rapidly and competition is ever-increasing, the ability to not just gather but also intelligently interpret online customer data is what sets successful businesses apart. This interpretation, often facilitated by advanced web analytics, allows companies to decode the complex patterns of customer behavior and preferences. The insights gained through such analysis are not merely numbers and trends; they are the guiding forces behind strategic decision-making, enabling businesses to craft experiences and products that resonate deeply with their target audience. As such, the role of web analytics extends beyond mere data collection – it involves understanding the story behind the data, the human element that transforms raw numbers into actionable insights.

However, the vast amount of data available through web analytics presents its own set of challenges. In a world awash with information, the key to efficacy lies in the ability to segment this data into meaningful and manageable categories. Proper segmentation allows businesses to identify and understand distinct customer groups, each with their unique behaviors, needs, and potential value to the company. This segmentation is not static; it evolves as customer behaviors and market dynamics change. Thus, businesses must continually adapt their segmentation strategies to stay relevant and effective. This dynamic process requires not only sophisticated analytical tools but also a keen understanding of market trends, consumer psychology, and the ever-changing digital environment.

Moreover, the power of online customer segmentation lies in its ability to personalize at scale. In an era where consumers are bombarded with generic advertising and content, personalized experiences stand out. They create a connection, foster loyalty, and drive engagement. By leveraging segmentation, businesses can deliver highly targeted marketing campaigns, develop products that address specific customer needs, and provide services that truly resonate with each segment. This level of personalization was once the domain of small, niche businesses, but with the advancements in web analytics, even large-scale enterprises can now offer the personalized touch that customers crave. This chapter aims to explore how businesses can harness the power of online customer segmentation in web analytics to create more impactful, customer-centric strategies that thrive in the digital age.

7.2 The Significance of Customer Segmentation in Web Analytics

Foster Enhanced Personalization

- **Description**: Segmenting customers in web analytics enables businesses to create personalized online experiences. This involves tailoring website content, product recommendations, and marketing messages to meet the unique preferences of different user groups.
- **Example**: An online bookstore uses web analytics to segment its audience based on their browsing history and past purchases. For each segment, the bookstore customizes its homepage to feature genres and titles that align with their interests, significantly enhancing user engagement and satisfaction.

Improve Engagement and Conversion

- **Description**: Targeted strategies developed through customer segmentation in web analytics can lead to higher engagement and conversion rates. By understanding and catering to the specific needs of each segment, businesses can create more compelling online experiences.
- **Example**: A SaaS company segments its website visitors based on their interaction patterns and page visits analyzed through web analytics. It then creates targeted pop-up messages offering a free trial to users who spend a significant amount of time on the pricing page, thereby increasing conversion rates.

Drive Informed Decisions

- **Description**: In-depth insights gained from web analytics-driven segmentation allow businesses to make data-driven decisions. This could pertain to marketing strategies, website design changes, or even broader business strategies.
- **Example**: An e-commerce platform uses web analytics to segment its customers based on their purchase frequency and average spend. Analyzing this data, the company decides to introduce a loyalty

program specifically targeting high-frequency, high-spend customers, thereby enhancing customer retention.

Inform Product Development

- **Description**: Customer segmentation through web analytics provides valuable insights for product development. By understanding the preferences and needs of different segments, businesses can develop or modify products to better cater to their market.
- **Example**: A video game developer uses web analytics to segment its players based on gameplay duration and in-game purchase behavior. This segmentation reveals a strong interest in certain in-game features among the most active users, guiding the developer to focus on enhancing these features in future updates.

7.3 Types of Segmentation in Web Analytics

Demographic Segmentation

- **Description**: Demographic segmentation categorizes customers based on age, gender, income, education level, and occupation. It is foundational in understanding the basic profile of website visitors. By analyzing these demographic factors, businesses can tailor their online presence to better suit different age groups or genders.
- **Data Collection**: This type of data is typically collected through user profiles, sign-up forms, or inferred through online behaviors and preferences. Web analytics tools track these demographics, often integrating with CRM systems for a more detailed customer profile.
- **Example**: An online retailer analyzes demographic data from their user sign-up forms and finds a strong presence of young, urban females on their site. They then customize their product range and marketing messages to cater to this demographic, leading to a significant increase in engagement and sales.

Geographic Segmentation

- **Description**: Geographic segmentation involves categorizing users by their location, from broad regions to specific cities. This type of segmentation is valuable for tailoring content and products to regional preferences or climate-specific needs.

- **Data Collection**: Geographic data is usually collected via IP addresses or location services on mobile devices. Web analytics tools can track and analyze user location to provide insights into regional trends and preferences.
- **Example**: A multinational e-commerce platform uses geographic data to segment its audience by region. They notice distinct purchasing patterns in different areas, leading them to tailor their inventory and marketing strategies regionally, significantly improving the user experience and sales in each locale.

Behavioral Segmentation

- **Description**: Behavioral segmentation focuses on user interactions with a website, including browsing patterns, purchase history, and engagement. This segmentation offers insights into user preferences and habits.
- **Data Collection**: Behavioral data is collected through website interaction tracking, such as pages visited, items added to a cart, and purchase history. This data is gathered and analyzed using web analytics tools to identify patterns and segment users accordingly.
- **Example**: A streaming platform segments its audience based on viewing habits tracked through their service. They create personalized watch lists and recommendations, leading to increased viewer engagement and higher subscription renewal rates.

Psychographic Segmentation

- **Description**: Psychographic segmentation dives into customers' lifestyles, interests, values, and attitudes. It aligns content and offers with the intrinsic motivations of the audience.
- **Data Collection**: This data is often collected through surveys, social media interactions, and behavior analysis on the website. Web analytics tools help in correlating this data with user activity to form psychographic profiles.
- **Example**: A lifestyle blog uses survey data and website interaction patterns to identify a segment interested in sustainable living. They focus their content on eco-friendly practices and green products, resulting in higher engagement and loyalty within this group.

Technographic Segmentation

- **Description**: Technographic segmentation categorizes users based on their technology usage, such as device type or browser preferences. This information is vital for optimizing user experience and understanding the technological preferences of the audience.
- **Data Collection**: Technographic data is collected by tracking the devices, operating systems, and browsers users employ to access the website. This tracking is typically done through web analytics tools that identify and segment users based on their technology usage.
- **Example**: An online software store analyzes data on the devices and browsers used by their visitors. Finding a trend towards high-end devices and the latest browsers, they adapt their product offerings and marketing to appeal to a tech-savvy customer base, leading to increased sales and customer satisfaction.

7.4 Buyer Personas to Customer Segments

A buyer persona is an essential tool in digital marketing and web analytics for generating effective customer segmentation groups. Essentially, a buyer persona is a semi-fictional representation of your ideal customer based on market research and real data about your existing customers. By creating detailed buyer personas, analysts and marketers can better understand their target audience, which in turn helps in forming more accurate and relevant customer segmentation groups. Here is how a buyer persona facilitates this process:

Understanding Target Audience

1. **Detailed Demographics**: Buyer personas include detailed demographic information such as age, gender, income level, and education. This detailed demographic profiling helps analysts segment the audience more precisely in their web analytics platforms.
2. **Behavioral Insights**: Buyer personas often outline typical behaviors, preferences, and buying habits of the target customer. These insights are crucial for behavioral segmentation, allowing analysts to categorize users based on their interactions with the website or product.

Enhancing Relevance and Personalization

3. **Personalized Marketing Efforts**: Knowing the specific characteristics of a buyer persona enables marketers to tailor their content and marketing strategies to meet the persona's needs and preferences, enhancing the effectiveness of targeted campaigns.
4. **Product Development and Positioning**: Understanding the buyer persona's preferences and pain points assists in developing products or services that meet their specific needs, and in positioning these offerings effectively.

Driving Strategic Decisions

5. **Strategic Content Creation**: Buyer personas help in creating content strategies that resonate with each segment. Content can be tailored to address the specific interests, challenges, and motivations of each persona.
6. **Channel Optimization**: Knowing where a buyer persona spends their time (e.g., social media platforms, forums, email) helps in segmenting users based on their preferred channels, optimizing channel strategy.

Increasing Efficiency and ROI

7. **Focused Marketing and Reduced Waste**: By understanding the buyer persona, marketers can avoid spending resources on broad, ineffective strategies and instead focus on targeted approaches that are more likely to convert.
8. **Improved Customer Journey Mapping**: Buyer personas allow for a clearer understanding of the customer journey, helping analysts to segment users based on their stage in the buying process.

Continuous Improvement

9. **Feedback Loop for Refinement**: Buyer personas are not static; they evolve as more data becomes available. Continuous analysis of customer segments against these personas allows for ongoing refinement and adjustment of marketing strategies.

Example in Practice

Imagine a company selling eco-friendly home products. By developing a detailed buyer persona that includes environmentally conscious homeowners, concerned about sustainability, and active in online eco-friendly communities, the company can create targeted marketing campaigns. Web analytics can then segment users who fit this profile, based on their browsing habits (e.g., reading sustainability blogs), and their interaction with specific content related to eco-friendly living. This targeted approach not only increases the relevance of the company's marketing efforts but also enhances user engagement and conversion rates.

While personas are heavily used by marketing, they should be embraced across your entire organization. Buyer personas help teams allocate resources, attract leads, and understand what drives people to make purchases. They are the type of customer that reminds you why you got into marketing or sales in the first place.

Personas help answer the following questions:

1. What type of content is most likely to generate a response from a particular type of customer?
2. How does your ideal customer prefer to engage in the sales process?
3. What problems do customers need to solve, and how does your business help them?

Creating inbound marketing campaigns with personas in mind focuses your efforts and boosts your ROI.

Persona development helps you determine:

- Which format(s) will generate the most interest
- Which media channels will reach the greatest number of prospective customers?
- The tone you should use when communicating with customers or writing content.
- The types of content most likely to attract new leads.
- Those calls to action with the highest response rate

Overall, a buyer persona is a valuable tool for companies to better understand and target their ideal customers, and to create marketing and sales strategies that are tailored to their needs and preferences.

To build a buyer persona, follow these steps:

1. **Define your target audience:** Start by identifying the customer segments that you want to target with your marketing and sales efforts. Consider factors such as demographics, behaviors, needs, and preferences.
2. **Gather data**: Collect data about your target audience through market research, customer surveys, focus groups, and other methods. Look for patterns and trends in the data and use it to create a detailed and accurate representation of your ideal customer.
3. **Create a detailed profile:** Use the data you have collected to create a detailed profile of your ideal customer. Include information about the persona's demographics, goals, challenges, and pain points, as well as their preferred channels of communication and decision-making process.
4. **Give your persona a name and a face:** Giving your persona a name and a face can help bring it to life and make it easier for your team to visualize and relate to. You can create a visual representation of your persona using a stock photo or a sketch.
5. **Review and update regularly:** Your buyer persona should be a living document that is reviewed and updated regularly to ensure that it remains accurate and relevant. As your business and customer base evolve, make sure to update your buyer persona to reflect any changes.

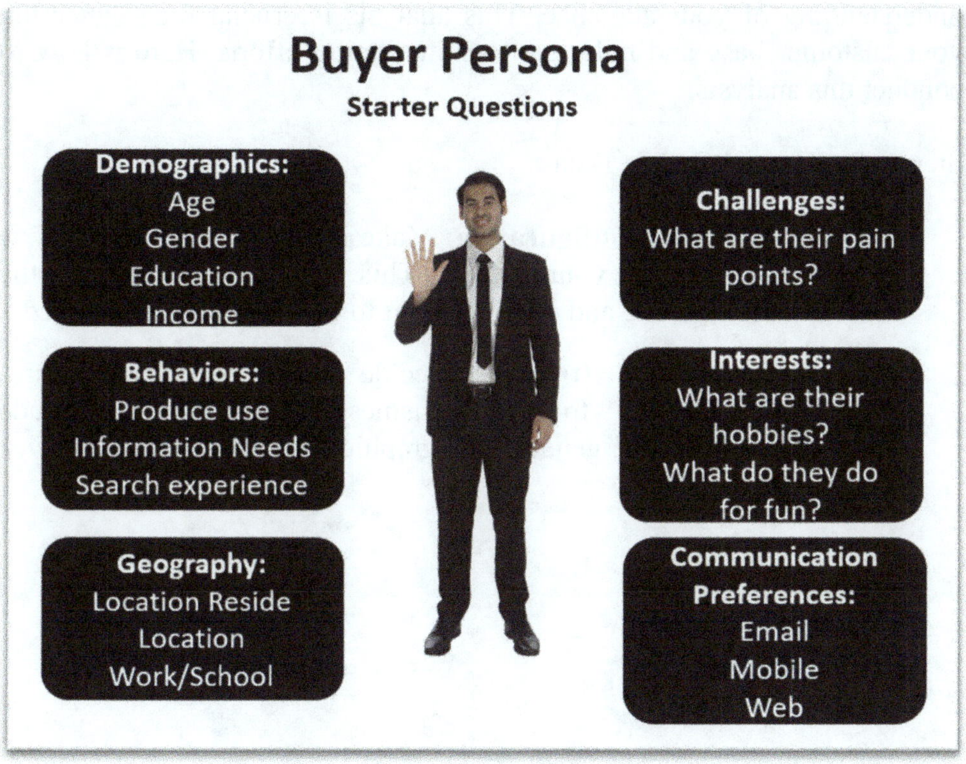

Figure 7.1 Buyer Persona Framework

The figure above displays the framework to get down to the persona of the target customer, starts with asking the level of starter questions to truly go down a path of analysis and research. The strongest buyer personas are ones that have taken the time to deep dive into the customer data and truly look beyond descriptive data, the patterns and trends of the behaviors and interests of the customers. We are also looking for what our product or service solves or gives to this persona. This way we can identify the best way to market those solutions and value propositions based on those pain points.

Lastly, we can group our customers into categories to further build out targeted marketing efforts for those who fit these characteristics. Whether they live in a certain region for location marketing, or we are focusing on their preferences on which digital channel to communicate, understanding the "ideal" customer with a buyer persona is a critical element of web and digital strategy.

7.5 Customer Attributes Analysis in Google Analytics 4

Customer attributes analysis in Google Analytics 4 (GA4) involves examining various characteristics of your website's users to gain a deeper understanding of your audience. This analysis is crucial for segmenting your customer base and tailoring your marketing efforts. Here is how to conduct this analysis:

Step 1: Set Up and Collect Data

- **Ensure Proper Configuration**: Make sure your GA4 property is correctly set up on your website. This involves implementing the GA4 tracking code and configuring it to collect the data you need.
- **Define Customer Attributes**: Decide on the customer attributes that are relevant to your business. These could include demographics (age, gender), geographic location, interests, device type, etc.

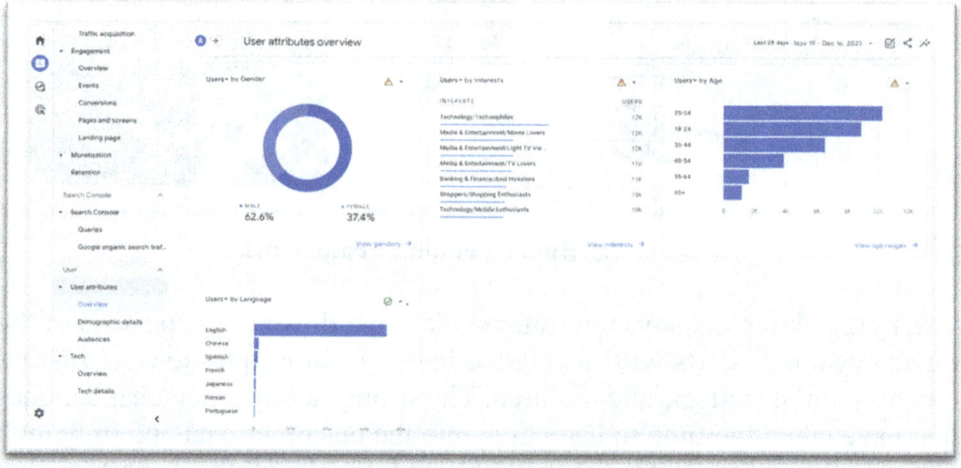

Figure 7.2 Google Analytics 4 User Attributes

Step 2: Accessing Reports

- **Navigate to User Reports**: In GA4, go to the 'Reports' section and explore the 'User' reports to view data related to user attributes.
- **Use Audience Builder**: Utilize GA4's Audience Builder to create custom audiences based on specific attributes. This tool allows you to combine various attributes and metrics to define your audience segments.

Search...   Rows per page: 10   Go to: 1   1-10 of 11

	Audience	Users	New users	Sessions	Views per session	Average session duration	Total revenue
		81,857 100% of total	192,633 100% of total	117,605 100% of total	18.77 Avg 0%	19m 23s Avg 0%	$1,011,618.03 100% of total
1	All Users	81,857	69,041	117,605	4.20	4m 35s	$193,323.13
2	Non-purchasers	81,857	69,041	117,605	4.20	4m 35s	$684.40
3	Recently active users	54,566	41,650	83,324	5.37	5m 22s	$193,323.13
4	Engaged Users	21,824	11,824	43,962	8.66	8m 08s	$193,195.73
5	Added to cart & no purchase	6,805	38	14,173	10.70	9m 01s	$0.00
6	Likely 7-day purchasers	5,094	25	15,618	6.12	6m 44s	$97,975.75
7	Predicted 28-day top spenders	2,875	22	8,525	6.23	7m 04s	$60,790.34
8	Top spenders: Top 5% of users	2,875	22	8,525	6.23	7m 04s	$60,790.34
9	Purchasers	1,558	0	3,511	5.37	6m 04s	$193,323.13
10	Users in San Francisco	1,535	970	2,841	6.50	6m 45s	$16,776.28

Step 3: Analyze Customer Data

- **Demographic Analysis**: Review demographic data like age and gender to understand the composition of your audience.
- **Geographic Analysis**: Examine where your users are coming from to identify popular regions or cities.
- **Interests and Behavior**: Look into the interests, browsing behavior, and purchase history of your users to understand what drives them.
- **Technographic Analysis**: Analyze the technology used by your audience, such as device type, operating system, and browser.

Step 4: Utilize Enhanced Measurement

- **Enable Enhanced Measurement**: In GA4, make sure Enhanced Measurement is turned on. This feature automatically collects data on various interactions like scrolls, outbound clicks, site search, etc., which can provide additional insights into user behavior.

Step 5: Review and Interpret Data

- **Synthesize Findings**: Compile the data into actionable insights. Look for trends and patterns that help you understand your audience better.
- **Regular Updates**: Customer attributes can change over time, so it is important to regularly review and update your analysis.

Conducting a customer attributes analysis in GA4 is not just about gathering data; it is about transforming that data into meaningful customer segments. Here is how this analysis contributes to building effective customer segments:

Identifying Core Segments: By analyzing customer attributes, you can identify core segments of your audience. For instance, you might find that a significant portion of your audience is millennials who are interested in technology.

Tailoring Marketing Strategies: Understanding the specific attributes of these segments allows you to tailor your marketing strategies. For the tech-savvy millennial segment, you might focus on digital marketing campaigns that leverage the latest tech trends.

Personalizing User Experience: With detailed knowledge of customer attributes, you can personalize the user experience on your website. Customization can range from personalized product recommendations to tailored content that resonates with each segment.

Optimizing Product Offerings: Analysis of customer attributes can inform product development and optimization. By understanding the needs and preferences of different segments, you can adapt your product offerings to better meet these demands.

Enhancing Customer Journey Mapping: Knowing the attributes of your customers helps in mapping out the customer journey more accurately. This knowledge enables you to engage with your customers more effectively at each stage of their journey.

Predictive Analysis: Over time, as you collect and analyze more data, you can use customer attributes to predict future trends and behaviors, helping you to stay ahead in your market.

Audience Building and Segmentation in GA4

Google Analytics 4 (GA4) introduces a more intuitive and flexible approach to audience building and segmentation, a vital aspect for any advertiser aiming to target their campaigns more effectively. Unlike its predecessor, GA4 operates on an event-based data model, which allows for a more granular understanding of user behavior.

The process of audience creation in GA4 starts with the identification of user attributes and behaviors that are most relevant to your advertising goals. These attributes could range from basic demographic information (age, gender, location) to more complex behavioral patterns (page views, purchase history, engagement levels). GA4's interface facilitates the combination of these attributes using 'and/or' conditions, allowing advertisers to create highly specific segments.

For instance, an e-commerce business can create an audience segment of users who viewed a product but did not make a purchase. Or a travel agency might focus on users who have shown interest in specific destinations or types of holidays. The key is to align these segments with your advertising goals, ensuring that the right message reaches the right audience at the right time.

Utilizing GA4's Audience Builder for Targeted Advertising

The Audience Builder tool in GA4 is a powerful feature for advertisers. It offers a user-friendly interface where segments can be built, edited, and immediately deployed in advertising campaigns. This tool allows for dynamic audience building, meaning the audience lists are automatically updated as users meet the criteria set by the advertiser.

For example, you can create an audience of users who have spent more than a certain amount of time on your site or have completed specific events, such as signing up for a newsletter. These audiences can then be directly linked to Google Ads, facilitating a seamless integration between analytics and advertising platforms.

One significant advantage of GA4's Audience Builder is its predictive capabilities. By leveraging machine learning, GA4 can predict future user behavior, such as the likelihood of a user making a purchase. Advertisers can use these predictions to create segments of users who are most likely to convert, optimizing the ROI of their ad campaigns.

Case Studies: Effective Audience Segmentation

Case Study 1: Online Retailer An online fashion retailer utilized GA4 to segment its audience based on purchasing behavior and browsing history. By creating a segment of users who viewed products in the 'summer collection' but did not make a purchase, the retailer was able to retarget these users with personalized ads and special offers. This strategy resulted in a 20% increase in conversions for the summer collection, displaying the effectiveness of precise audience segmentation in GA4.

Case Study 2: Travel Agency A travel agency leveraged GA4 to target users interested in luxury travel. They created segments based on users who spent time on pages related to luxury destinations and had a high engagement level. By targeting these users with tailored ads for exclusive travel packages, the agency saw a 30% increase in inquiries and a 15% increase in booking conversion rates.

Case Study 3: Tech Company A tech company used GA4 to identify and retarget users who visited their website but did not download their whitepaper. They segmented users based on the time spent on specific content pages and retargeted them with direct email campaigns and personalized ads. This led to a 40% increase in whitepaper downloads and a significant boost in user engagement.

Conclusion

Audience building and segmentation in GA4 offer unparalleled flexibility and depth for advertisers. By effectively utilizing the Audience Builder and leveraging the predictive power of GA4, advertisers can create highly targeted campaigns that resonate with their intended audience. The real-world case studies illustrate how diverse businesses have successfully implemented these strategies, resulting in improved engagement, higher conversion rates, and ultimately, a better return on advertising investment. As GA4 continues to evolve, it is clear that its audience segmentation capabilities will become an even more critical tool for digital advertisers.

Key Points:

1. Online customer segmentation and analysis are essential in today's digital landscape to interpret customer data intelligently.
2. Proper segmentation helps identify distinct customer groups with unique behaviors and needs.
3. Online customer segmentation enables personalized marketing, improved engagement, and informed decision-making.
4. Several types of segmentation in web analytics include demographic, geographic, behavioral, psychographic, and technographic.
5. Buyer personas play a crucial role in effective customer segmentation by providing detailed insights into target audiences.
6. Customer attributes analysis in Google Analytics 4 involves examining user characteristics to gain a deeper understanding of the audience.
7. This analysis contributes to building effective customer segments, tailoring marketing strategies, personalizing user experiences, and optimizing product offerings.

Discussion Questions:

1. How does online customer segmentation help businesses create more personalized and engaging online experiences for their customers?
2. What challenges do businesses face when trying to segment their online customer data effectively, and how can they overcome these challenges?
3. Can you provide examples of businesses that have successfully used online customer segmentation to enhance their marketing strategies and customer engagement?
4. What are the key differences between demographic, geographic, behavioral, psychographic, and technographic segmentation in web analytics, and when is each type most useful?
5. How can businesses ensure that their buyer personas accurately represent their target audience and remain relevant over time?

Chapter Eight: Web Promotions & Performance Measurement

8.1 Introduction

As the digital marketplace continues to evolve and expand, the strategic importance of web promotions analytics in the field of digital marketing has become increasingly prominent. In this high-paced and competitive environment, businesses are constantly seeking innovative ways to capture the attention of their target audience, drive engagement, and ultimately boost sales. The key to achieving these objectives lies in the effective utilization of web promotions analytics—a multifaceted tool that empowers businesses to decode the complexities of online promotional activities.

Web promotions analytics is an intricate process that involves more than just the superficial monitoring of campaign performance metrics. It is an in-depth analytical approach to understanding, tracking, and refining the efficacy of various online marketing initiatives and promotional events. This analytical process encompasses a broad spectrum of activities, from scrutinizing user engagement patterns and conversion rates to evaluating the return on investment (ROI) for different marketing strategies. At the heart of web promotions analytics is the goal to extract actionable insights from data—insights that can guide future marketing decisions, enable the optimization of promotional efforts, and drive sustainable business growth.

This chapter serves as an essential guide, meticulously exploring the realm of web promotions analytics. It begins by shedding light on what web promotions analytics entails, underpinning its fundamental principles and objectives. We will navigate through the nuances of various online marketing campaigns and promotional events, understanding their unique characteristics and the critical role they play in a business's digital marketing strategy. These promotional activities range from time-sensitive deals and flash sales to comprehensive annual events and meticulously planned email marketing campaigns. Each of these promotions has its own set of goals, challenges, and metrics that need to be analyzed for a comprehensive understanding of their performance.

As we delve deeper into the chapter, we will discuss how to methodically analyze and optimize these web promotions. This includes a detailed examination of the types of data that should be collected and the key performance indicators (KPIs) that need to be measured. We will explore various analytical tools and techniques used in the industry, providing insights into how businesses can harness this data to make informed decisions. The discussion will extend to understanding customer behavior through segmentation and mapping the customer journey, crucial steps in personalizing and enhancing the customer experience.

Moreover, the chapter will address the importance of testing and optimization in the realm of web promotions. Techniques such as A/B testing and continuous iterative improvements will be highlighted, highlighting their significance in refining marketing strategies and promotional campaigns for maximum impact.

The journey through this chapter will equip readers with a comprehensive understanding of web promotions analytics. It aims to provide a foundation for marketers, analysts, and business leaders to effectively leverage web promotions analytics, transforming data into actionable strategies that resonate with their audience, optimize promotional efforts, and contribute to the overarching goals of their business in the digital marketplace.

8.2 Understanding Web Promotions

Web promotions are strategic marketing campaigns executed online, designed to attract, engage, and convert a digital audience. These promotions harness the capabilities of the digital landscape—spanning across websites, social media, email campaigns, and online advertisements—to deliver enticing offers to a broad yet targeted demographic. They are pivotal in boosting brand awareness, stimulating sales, and fostering customer loyalty in a highly competitive online market.

The strength of web promotions lies in their dual value proposition. For consumers, they offer tangible benefits like discounts, exclusive access, or unique opportunities. For businesses, these promotions drive increased traffic, accelerate sales, and provide valuable insights into customer preferences and behavior. Effective web promotions are not just about short-term gains; they play a significant role in long-term brand building and customer relationship management.

Types of Web Promotions

1. Deal of the Day

- **Description**: 'Deal of the Day' promotions create a sense of urgency by offering significant discounts on specific products or services, but only for a 24-hour window. These deals are often used to clear inventory, introduce new products, or attract new customers.

- **Immediacy of Analysis**: Analysis should be rapid and focused, as these promotions have a very short lifespan. It is crucial to evaluate the impact immediately after the promotion ends to understand its effectiveness and prepare for future deals.
- **What to Assess**: Key metrics include sales volume, new versus returning customers, website traffic and engagement during the promotion period, and the performance of marketing channels in driving traffic.

2. Seasonal Events

- **Description**: Tied to particular seasons or holidays, seasonal events can last several weeks and often involve thematic promotions. These campaigns are critical for businesses due to their potential to drive significant sales volumes, such as holiday shopping seasons.
- **Immediacy of Analysis**: Continuous analysis throughout the event is essential, with a comprehensive review post-event to assess overall performance.
- **What to Assess**: Track overall sales, customer engagement trends, effectiveness of marketing campaigns across different channels, inventory turnover, and compare the performance with non-seasonal periods.

3. Annual Events

- **Description**: Events like Black Friday and Cyber Monday represent key dates in the retail calendar, featuring wide-ranging discounts. They require extensive planning and often serve as a significant revenue driver for the year.
- **Immediacy of Analysis**: Real-time monitoring during the event is crucial, alongside a detailed post-event analysis to evaluate success and inform future strategies.
- **What to Assess**: Examine year-over-year performance, customer traffic patterns, conversion rates, average order values, and the ROI of various promotional channels.

4. Weekly/Weekend Sales

- **Description**: Regular sales events, such as weekend discounts, offer opportunities to boost sales during typically slower periods. These promotions can also be used to test new marketing strategies.
- **Immediacy of Analysis**: Prompt post-event analysis is vital due to the recurring nature of these sales, allowing for adjustments and improvements for future iterations.
- **What to Assess**: Focus on comparing weekend and weekday performance, customer buying behavior, effectiveness of promotional messaging, and any variations in average purchase values.

5. Flash Sales

- **Description**: Flash sales are high-energy, short-term promotions designed to drive immediate action. They often feature steep discounts and are a powerful tool for quick inventory turnover and customer acquisition.
- **Immediacy of Analysis**: Instant analysis is necessary due to the fleeting nature of these sales. Rapid response and adaptability are key to capitalizing on the insights gained.
- **What to Assess**: Monitor immediate spikes in traffic, conversion rate fluctuations during the sale period, the efficacy of different marketing channels in driving urgent purchases, and inventory levels before and after the sale.

6. Loyalty Program Promotions

- **Description**: These promotions are targeted at existing customers, rewarding them for their loyalty with exclusive deals or points. They are crucial for maintaining long-term customer relationships and encouraging repeat business.
- **Immediacy of Analysis**: This requires a more extended analysis period, focusing on long-term customer engagement and retention.
- **What to Assess**: Evaluate customer retention rates, frequency of repeat purchases, the effectiveness of various loyalty rewards in driving purchases, and overall customer lifetime value.

In summary, each type of web promotion demands a distinct approach in terms of execution and analysis. Understanding the unique elements of these various promotions enables businesses to devise more effective marketing strategies and extract valuable insights from their promotional activities. The immediacy and focus of analysis vary across promotion types, underscoring the need for adaptable and responsive analytics practices to fully harness the potential of each promotional campaign.

8.3 Promotional vs Baseline Sales

Introduction In the digital commerce landscape, distinguishing between promotional and baseline sales, including advertising expenses, is key to evaluating the effectiveness of online marketing campaigns and shaping strategic business decisions. This distinction helps in understanding the true impact of promotional activities, including advertising costs, on overall sales performance.

Understanding Promotional and Baseline Sales

- **Promotional Sales:** These represent the additional sales volume generated directly from marketing campaigns or promotional events, including advertising expenses. Promotional sales spike during periods when businesses offer special deals, discounts, or other incentives to stimulate consumer interest and drive purchases.
- **Baseline Sales:** Baseline sales are the regular sales volume a business achieves without the influence of special promotions or marketing efforts, taking into account advertising costs. This figure is the normative benchmark for sales, representing the consistent, day-to-day sales performance of the business.

Calculating Promotional vs. Baseline Sales The calculation involves establishing a baseline sales figure, considering advertising expenses, and then measuring the increase in sales during promotional periods, accounting for advertising costs. The process can be outlined as follows:

1. **Establish Baseline Sales:** Analyze historical sales data during periods without promotions and factor in advertising expenses to find the average sales volume. This average represents your baseline sales, taking into account the costs of advertising.
2. **Measure Total Sales During Promotion:** Record the total sales volume during the promotional period, considering advertising expenses as part of the promotion costs.

3. **Calculate Promotional Sales:** Subtract the baseline sales, accounting for advertising expenses, from the total sales during the promotional period, including advertising costs. The resultant figure represents the sales attributable to the promotion, factoring in advertising expenses.

Formula: Promotional Sales (Including Advertising Expense) = Total Sales during Promotion (Including Advertising Cost) - Baseline Sales (Including Advertising Cost)

Examples with Calculation

Example 1: Weekend Flash Sale

- Baseline Sales (Average Daily Sales, including advertising costs): $2,500
- Total Sales during Weekend Flash Sale (2 Days, including advertising cost): $6,500
- Promotional Sales Calculation: $6,500 - ($2,500 x 2 days) = $6,500 - $5,000 = $1,500
- Interpretation: The weekend flash sale, including advertising costs, generated an additional $1,500 in sales over the typical weekend performance, accounting for advertising expenses.

Example 2: Black Friday Event

- Baseline Sales (Average Daily Sales, including advertising costs): $3,500
- Total Sales on Black Friday (including advertising cost): $10,500
- Promotional Sales Calculation: $10,500 - $3,500 = $7,000
- Interpretation: The Black Friday event, including advertising costs, led to an increase in sales by $7,000 compared to a regular day's sales, taking into account advertising expenses.

Example 3: Email Marketing Campaign

- Baseline Sales (Average Weekly Sales, including advertising costs): $16,500

- Total Sales during Week of Email Campaign (including advertising cost): $23,500
- Promotional Sales Calculation: $23,500 - $16,500 = $7,000
- Interpretation: The week-long email marketing campaign, including advertising expenses, resulted in an additional $7,000 in sales, factoring in advertising costs.

Importance in E-commerce Strategy

- **Evaluating Campaign Effectiveness:** This analysis, including advertising expenses, helps in quantitatively assessing the impact of different promotional strategies, guiding decisions on where to invest marketing resources for maximum returns.
- **Strategic Decision-Making:** Understanding promotional vs. baseline sales, including advertising costs, aids in strategic planning, from determining the timing and nature of future promotions to resource allocation.
- **Inventory Management:** Accurate predictions based on this analysis, including advertising expenses, can guide inventory stocking decisions, ensuring adequate supply during promotional periods without overstocking.
- **Customer Buying Behavior Insights:** This analysis, including advertising costs, sheds light on customer responsiveness to various promotions, revealing insights into consumer behavior and preferences.
- **Long-Term Business Growth Trends:** By consistently analyzing promotional and baseline sales, including advertising expenses, businesses can track their growth trajectory and assess whether it is driven by promotions or organic sales increase.

In summary, the analysis of promotional versus baseline sales, while considering advertising expenses, provides a comprehensive understanding of the effectiveness of marketing campaigns in e-commerce. It serves as a critical tool for businesses to optimize their promotional strategies, manage resources efficiently, and gain valuable insights into customer behavior and long-term growth trends, factoring in advertising costs.

8.4 Promotions Analytics in Google Analytics 4

Analyzing promotions in Google Analytics 4 (GA4) involves a few steps to properly track and evaluate the performance of your promotional campaigns.

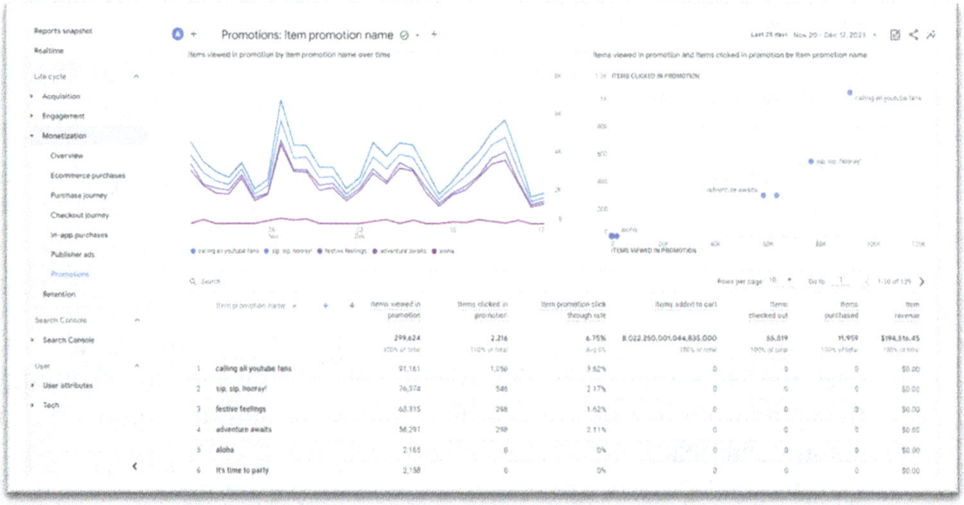

Figure 8.1 Google Analytics 4 Promotions View

Here is a general guide on how to go about it:

1. **Set Up Your Tracking**: Before analyzing promotions, ensure that you have set up you are tracking correctly. This involves tagging your promotional links or ads with UTM parameters. These parameters allow GA4 to identify the source, medium, campaign, and other details of the traffic coming to your website.

2. **Access Google Analytics 4**: Log in to your Google Analytics 4 account.

3. **Navigate to the Reports Section**: In GA4, you will find most of your data under the “Reports” section. Here, you can access a variety of pre-built reports or create custom reports.

4. **Analyze Acquisition Reports**: In the “Acquisition” reports, look for the “Traffic Acquisition” report. This report will show you how users are coming to your site, including those coming through your promotions.

5. **Look for UTM Parameters**: In the Traffic Acquisition report, you can filter by the UTM parameters you have set up. This will allow

you to see data specifically for your promotional campaigns, like the number of users, sessions, and the bounce rate.

6. **Check User Engagement**: To understand how users are interacting with your site after clicking on a promotion, navigate to the "Engagement" section. Here, you can analyze metrics like pages per session, average session duration, and event count.

7. **Evaluate Conversions**: If you have set up conversion events in GA4, you can analyze how your promotions are contributing to conversions. Go to the "Conversions" section to see data on completed goals.

8. **Use Explorations**: For deeper analysis, use the "Explorations" feature in GA4. This allows you to create custom reports and segment data in various ways, giving you a more detailed view of how your promotions are performing.

9. **Compare Data**: To understand the effectiveness of different promotions, compare the data from different time periods, or between different campaigns using the comparison feature in GA4.

10. **Monitor Real-Time Data**: The "Realtime" report in GA4 can be used to monitor the immediate impact of your promotions.

11. **Create Custom Dashboards**: For a quicker view of your promotional data, you might want to set up custom dashboards within GA4. This allows you to see the most relevant data at a glance.

12. **Regularly Review and Adjust**: Regularly check your promotional data in GA4 to understand what is working and what is not. Use these insights to adjust your promotional strategies for better results.

Remember, the key to effective analysis in GA4 is to clearly define what you want to track and regularly review the data to gain insights into your promotional campaigns' performance. Additionally, GA4 is constantly evolving, so keep an eye on new features and updates that can enhance your analysis.

Key Points:

1. Web promotions analytics plays a crucial role in digital marketing by helping businesses attract, engage, and convert their target audience effectively.
2. Web promotions analytics goes beyond monitoring metrics and involves in-depth analysis to extract actionable insights for future marketing decisions.
3. Several types of web promotions include Deal of the Day, Seasonal Events, Annual Events, Weekly/Weekend Sales, Flash Sales, and Loyalty Program Promotions.
4. Distinguishing between promotional and baseline sales, including advertising expenses, is essential for evaluating the effectiveness of online marketing campaigns.
5. The calculation of promotional vs. baseline sales involves establishing a baseline, measuring total sales during promotions, calculating promotional sales, factoring in advertising costs.
6. Analyzing promotions in Google Analytics 4 (GA4) requires setting up tracking, accessing the reports section, analyzing acquisition, engagement, and conversion reports, using explorations for deeper analysis, and regularly reviewing and adjusting your data.
7. GA4 allows businesses to track the performance of their promotional campaigns and gain insights into user behavior, traffic sources, and conversion rates.

Discussion Questions:

1. How can businesses use web promotions analytics to measure the effectiveness of their online marketing campaigns and make data-driven decisions?
2. What are the key benefits of distinguishing between promotional and baseline sales, including advertising expenses, in the context of e-commerce strategy?
3. Can you provide examples of businesses that have successfully leveraged web promotions analytics to boost their brand awareness, sales, and customer loyalty?
4. How does the choice of web promotion type (e.g., flash sales vs. loyalty program promotions) impact the analysis and evaluation process, including the assessment of advertising expenses?
5. What are the challenges and considerations when setting up tracking and analyzing promotions in Google Analytics 4, and how can businesses overcome them?

Chapter Nine: Digital Content Analysis

9.1 Introduction

In today's digital age, the importance of digital content in web analytics cannot be overstated. Web analytics is the process of collecting, measuring, and analyzing data related to website traffic and user behavior. Digital content plays a pivotal role in this field as it serves as the foundation upon which web analytics operates. In this five-paragraph introduction, we will delve into the multifaceted significance of digital content in the realm of web analytics.

First and foremost, digital content is the lifeblood of any website. It encompasses everything from text and images to videos and interactive elements. The quality, relevance, and engagement level of this content directly influences how visitors interact with a website. By closely examining user interactions with different types of content, web analysts can gain insights into user preferences, needs, and behaviors. This information is invaluable for optimizing a website's content strategy to cater to the target audience effectively.

Secondly, digital content is a primary driver of traffic to a website. Search engines, social media platforms, and other online channels rely on content to index and rank websites. Effective search engine optimization (SEO) strategies revolve around creating high-quality, keyword-rich content that attracts organic traffic. Web analytics tools can track the performance of various content pieces, helping website owners identify which pages or pieces of content are driving the most traffic and conversions. This data informs content creators about what resonates with their audience and allows them to refine their content strategies accordingly.

Furthermore, digital content serves as the medium through which businesses and organizations convey their messages and offerings to their target audience. The effectiveness of this communication can be measured through web analytics, which tracks how users engage with content, including bounce rates, time spent on pages, click-through rates, and conversion rates. Understanding these metrics enables organizations to refine their content to better align with their goals, whether it is to educate, inform, entertain, or sell products and services.

In addition to the impact on user behavior, digital content also affects key performance indicators (KPIs) such as website traffic, user retention, and conversion rates. Analyzing the performance of content elements allows businesses to make data-driven decisions. For instance, if a specific blog post consistently drives more leads or sales than others, businesses can invest more in creating similar content to capitalize on its success. Conversely, if certain content types or pages underperform, adjustments can be made to enhance their effectiveness.

9.2 Content Marketing Strategy

Figure 9.1 Content Marketing Strategy

Content marketing is more than just generating and distributing content. It is a comprehensive strategy for attracting and engaging a certain audience and, eventually, generating lucrative consumer interaction. The four essential aspects of a successful content marketing strategy are the brand positioning, the owned media value proposition, the business case, and the strategic plan. Let us now look at why each of these aspects is important for content marketing and how they can be used.

A key element of any content marketing strategy is ensuring the content's ability to resonate with its audience. Content can be anything from messaging or imagery to how an advertisement is displayed with regard to the user interface and experience. With that in mind, we should remember that this does not only concern what is being said—how it is said is equally as important. For this reason, it is crucial to focus both on the visual aspect of how a message is conveyed (which should be done in a way that retains attention) and also the credibility of what is actually being said. Behavioral digital analytics should evaluate both aspects of these goals within content marketing.

Content marketing focuses on detailing to consumers and stakeholders what a brand or product is and what it stands for. What sets some companies apart from others is that their content resonates better with consumers. A key point here is also differentiating between the content itself and the copy's ability to perform in an SEO setting. Measuring behavioral metrics (e.g., clicks, views, and impressions) can help in evaluating this. The amount of interaction with the content can often indicate whether it is resonating with consumers. In an ideal case, the product or service will address a problem that the target market already faces. When this target audience begins to recognize and solve the problem, a company's content can guide and educate them.

An effective content strategy benefits users at both ends of the consumer life cycle: those who are still finding out what their key issues are; and those who are currently utilizing the product to tackle them. Good content supports the solution(s) the company is presenting and qualifies consumers to utilize the product more effectively. In essence, the customer's values and their needs should be the forefront of content marketing strategies. This relates to a customer-centric viewpoint in that the content should resonate with the customer.

9.3 Content Marketing Analysis

A comprehensive content marketing analysis is a critical aspect of understanding the effectiveness of a company's or its competitor's content strategy. This assessment not only aids in shaping the company's branding but also ensures a competitive perspective is maintained. It provides valuable insights into industry dynamics. Companies can conduct in-depth content marketing research or focus on specific elements to gauge their competitiveness. It is worth noting that while some may view analyzing competitors' materials as "copycatting," the information obtained through this approach is typically public and not confidential.

The process of effective content marketing analysis follows a structured series of steps. It commences with market research, where thorough preparation is paramount. The foundation of a research strategy hinges on its initial conception and evolution. Therefore, content analysis plays a pivotal role in this phase. It begins by compiling a comprehensive list of all published content, which is then meticulously scrutinized. Utilizing a content management system is essential for categorizing each aspect of the website, including links, videos, images, infographics, and audio. This segmentation helps identify issues, such as broken links or slow-loading images, thereby enhancing the overall customer experience. These seemingly minor details can significantly impact the website's success (Angel, 2015).

The subsequent step entails a thorough examination of the content to identify problems or inconsistencies on the website. Various techniques can be employed to collect this data, with direct consumer feedback often proving the most valuable. Selecting the right individuals to engage with and establishing effective communication methods is crucial in this regard.

Since content analysis rarely yields simple "yes" or "no" responses, internal examination becomes an essential next phase. Encouraging employees and managers to assess what they observe from within the organization is a valuable approach. During an internal review, alignment with the company's content and strategic goals should be the primary concern. Separating internal and external activities into distinct categories facilitates the detection of discrepancies. Paying close attention to customer reactions and their shared experiences is essential, especially noting key phrases that reflect their sentiments and the underlying reasons. Strong trends in responses often indicate areas where the company excels or falls short. Armed with this data, identifying strengths and weaknesses becomes more straightforward.

Content Marketing Metrics

Content-related metrics will correspond to specific goals for influencing user behavior. Advertising effectiveness is key when evaluating content marketing analysis. The fundamental objective of brand awareness is to get in front of customers' eyes. Notably, this is only half of the struggle; keeping their attention is the real problem. For example, one brand may have higher levels of domain authority over another brand. This alone does not guarantee that they have a high-level of brand awareness. Measuring the effectiveness of the chosen content helps ensure that the brand is kept relevant (i.e., in the mind of the consumer as they compare brands). Metrics for impressions, clicks, views, and other behavioral metrics would support this type of measurement. This may be determined by taking the several measurements, including

- **The number of customers who return to your site.** This can be measured by using customer profiles, repurchase choices, and other methods.

- **The number of customers who have**, for example, not placed a second order, cancelled subscriptions, or returned items.
- **Overall traffic.** Once traffic is built towards a website, the goal is for customers to interact with it in whatever manner they desire. Engagement is an indication that people feel connected to and engaged with our material, whether it is through positive interaction (e.g., upvotes or thumbs-up reactions), posting comments on articles, or copying the URL and sharing it elsewhere on the internet. Through these actions, customers are more likely to assist in driving even more visitors toward the website and optimizing the marketing funnel. While the widespread integration of social media has made tracking engagement opportunities easier than ever, it still makes sense to make those interaction options available without the site.

9.4 Content Marketing & The Digital Funnel

Top of the funnel (ToFu) content, middle of the funnel (MoFu) content, and bottom of the funnel (BoFu) content are the three forms of material commonly used by content marketing specialists. The funnel for each refers to the purchasing funnel, often known as the consumer journey, so far, which includes awareness, active evaluation, purchase, and post-purchase. We can simply trace each level of the funnel using RACE phases and consumer journey stages.

Top of the Funnel

ToFu content initiatives address the customer journey's awareness stage and align with the Reach stage. Consumers are feeling and expressing symptoms of a need, issue, or difficulty they are encountering at the awareness stage. The information is intended to educate them. The abstractness of the consumer's demand, problem, or difficulty might vary.

For example, they might be suffering from lower-back discomfort and seeking a cure. Or perhaps they require a new pair of running shoes. As a result, content should address problems in ways that correspond to what customers are experiencing. Content at the top of the funnel should educate and entertain customers based on their need, problem, or challenge. If consumers do not realize they need your product or comprehend what their problem is, you, as the marketer, must educate them.

Blog posts, webinars, pillar pages, and longer-form content such as thorough manuals, films, and infographics are examples of material that often help at this stage, though this is not an exhaustive or exclusive list.

Middle of the Funnel

MoFu content initiatives are aligned with the Act stage and target the active assessment step of the consumer experience. Consumers are eager to examine solutions during the active evaluation stage. Thus, content should directly address the solutions that customers may utilize to address their wants, issues, or challenges.

The objective of content at the middle of the funnel is to encourage active assessment and to function as a link between education and your product or service. It is still necessary to represent the customer and restrict persuasive attempts, but this must be balanced with warming customers gradually to what you have to offer. Content in the center of the funnel should assist customers in evaluating their alternatives and support that evaluation by educating and entertaining them on potential solutions. The goal at this point is to begin producing leads.

Bottom of the Funnel

BoFu content activities are aimed toward the buying stage and correspond to the Convert stage. Consumers are looking to buy a product during this stage. Content at this level should assist customers in evaluating your product or service to encourage them to purchase what you are offering over what rivals are offering.

Content at the bottom of the funnel should enlighten and persuade customers about your product or service. At this point, the firm's goal is to convert leads into customers. Testimonials and reviews, product offers, trials, discounts, samples, demos, free assessments or consultations, convincing product descriptions, and sales-oriented webinars are examples of material that generally help here, though this is not an exhaustive or exclusive list.

Figure 9.1 below provides an example of a consumer dilemma that their car is broken down. Their problem is clear, but the influence on which direction to go, whether to repair their car or buy a new one, is part of their problem identification.

In this scenario, imagine if this individual's car had 200,000 miles on it and they have already invested a lot of money in the past five years for repair. Versus, the other individual who just bought a car in the past three years with only 30,000 miles on it and this is their first major repair. Each of these examples have different thought processes. This is where each element of the funnel in content needs to consider the following from a potential customer's perspective in their decision making and thought process.

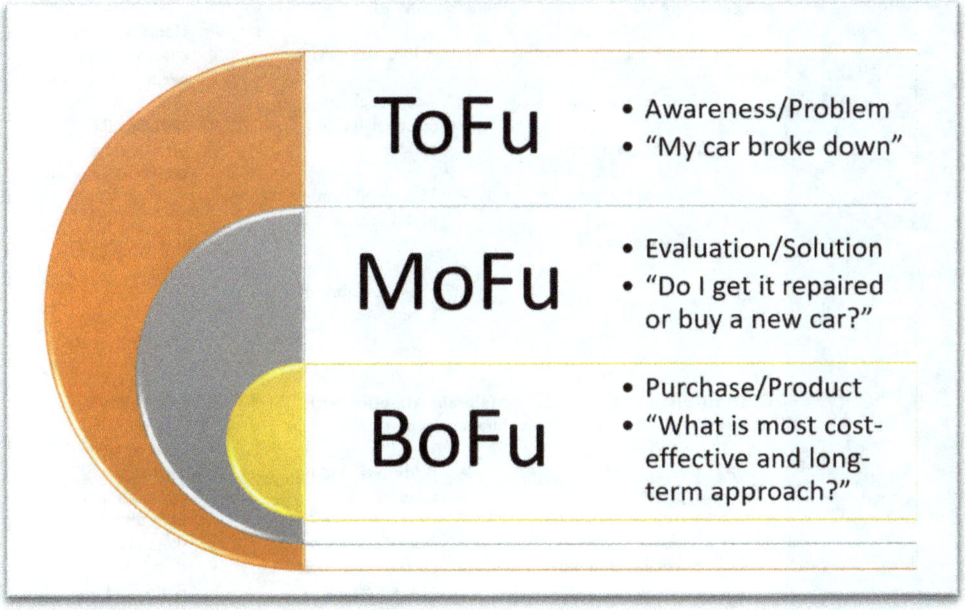

Figure 9.2 Consumer Decision Process in Digital Funnel, (Allison, 2022).

An initial view of a content strategy needs to clearly understand the problem or opportunity being presented. Next, how do we leverage the content to influence and educate the consumer on that problem or opportunity? Finally, how do we close or convert that consumer to ensure they have confidence and trust in that purchase? The right imagery, written material, and design all matter in each step. This next diagram considers even more detailed questions about how to approach the content in each step of the funnel.

Consumer Example	ToFu	MoFu	BoFu
Car with 200K miles	**Grab attention with imagery/copy of:** ➢ A new car ➢ Trade in program ➢ Pricing/Discounts ➢ New car feeling ➢ Lifestyle appeal	**Maintain Attention with imagery/copy of:** ➢ Additional services ➢ Additional discounts/pricing options ➢ The added features of the vehicle ➢ Other considerations of Evaluation	**Close the conversion:** ➢ Home in on the exact service needed ➢ Focus on the pricing value prop
Car with 30K Miles	**Grab attention with imagery/copy of:** ➢ Warranty info if applicable ➢ Repair discounts/promotions ➢ Supporting expertise on finding out "What is wrong"	**Maintain Attention with imagery/copy of:** ➢ Additional add-on features ➢ Added content to be clear on what part of the warranty is important ➢ Offer trust in the repair with specifics	**Close the conversion:** ➢ Final input on copy of the information to sway any skepticism ➢ Build final trust factors with the repair service ➢ Be clear and concise in the final steps

Figure 9.3 Example of Funnel Analysis

The figure above demonstrates the thought process a digital marketer would use and the type of imagery, aesthetics, and marketing copy to focus on in each step of the funnel in a customer's purchase decision process, garnering immediately attractive elements at the top and building trust, clarity, and confidence through the experience. Content generation and management is beyond just the initial impression. It carries through the entire experience with a customer and all thought processes, and considerations from a customer perspective need to be considered.

9.5 Content Types

There are three primary types of content in digital marketing: evergreen, organized, and topical.

- **Evergreen**: This is also known as flow material since it is not time-sensitive and can be used at any time. It may be planned and prepared months ahead of time, and it can be recycled and reused.

- **Organized**: Content is planned and created ahead of time. It is frequently linked to planned events in the organization's annual calendar, such as national days, seasonal celebrations, or product launches.
- **Topical:** Material includes noteworthy items. Includes current events, newsworthy and/or other high visibility information.

User Generated Content

Marketing is becoming more consumer centric as the power of success is in the hands of customers. Brands are developing opportunities for people to interact with, engage with, and advocate for their marketing initiatives. As a result, user-generated content is the recipe that marketers utilize to execute effective marketing campaigns.

User-generated content (UGC) refers to any type of content created and published by users based on their own experiences, views, ideas, or comments. Digital platforms, particularly social media networks, serve as a repository for user-generated content. In marketing, UGC is content that is relevant to the brand: online reviews, product images, consumer comments, product videos, and so on. UGC is recognized to be the most dependable, trustworthy, and authentic kind of content when compared to brand-pushed marketing material since it is experience-driven and honest. Marketers covet this rich user-generated content because of these qualities.

Why is user-generated content important for effective digital marketing?

1. Broad Reach and Exposure

The initial goal of any digital marketing plan should be to reach a large audience with significant exposure to maximize the possibilities of engagement and conversions. User participation in the campaign may assist a brand in meeting these objectives fast and efficiently. When you build a campaign with your unique brand hashtags, you can encourage consumers to express their thoughts and ideas on social media sites by using the hashtag. When users do so, it broadens the reach and visibility of your marketing campaign to a larger range of people without regard to demographics or geography.

2. Unique and Diverse Content

The key requirement for the effectiveness of every marketing effort is to produce creative and compelling content. You may employ user-generated content to harness varied and innovative material. Because there are only a limited number of minds at work while creating material in-house, the diversity and inventiveness of the content is constrained. However, there are many internet users with innovative ideas and opinions who create a varied spectrum of intriguing, engaging material.

3. Emphasizes Social Proof

Customers' social proof validates the brand's trustworthiness, authenticity, and dependability of its products and services. In this digital age, social proof is incredibly essential since it impacts consumer purchasing decisions. It will be impossible for your company to launch marketing efforts to establish social proof since customers will not trust self-promotion. As a result, UGC provides an ideal answer to this challenge. Making user-generated content a focal point of your marketing efforts can increase the reliability and trustworthiness of your promotional message and information, increasing user engagement and conversions.

4. Demonstrates Brand Advocacy

Brand advocacy occurs when people believe in a brand, demonstrate loyalty, and advocate for it to other consumers, i.e., talk positively about the brand. If your business has these committed customers or, even better, brand advocates, you can leverage their generated content to promote brand advocacy, which will aid in recruiting new consumers and income creation through existing customers' content. Including brand champions and their content in your marketing initiatives can also increase brand attractiveness among non-customers and help the business manage its image in the digital ecosystem. Brand advocacy demonstrates the brand's exceptional quality of goods and services while providing superior customer experience.

6. Increases Humanistic Approach

Humanizing your marketing involves using emotive and relationship-building factors. It is difficult to express the emotions that link customers with businesses through conventional brand marketing. However, user-generated content enables marketers to engage emotionally with their audiences, win their trust, demonstrate authenticity, and develop meaningful connections. UGC reveals how other consumers are experiencing your brand and eliciting feelings of empathy or even jealousy.

Using customer emotions to increase engagement and brand conversions offers long-term success.

7. Creates an Online Community

Humans build communities, whether small or large, with other people who have similar interests, likes, preferences, or consumption experiences of a brand's products or services. By using the material of your loyal customers or brand advocates, you may create an online community with your consumers. Harley-Davidson is a great example of a company with powerful internet communities. These communities assist in the creation of positive user-generated content about the brand in their networks, which increases traffic, user engagement, brand visibility, desirability, conversion possibilities, and brand advocacy.

8. Simple Content Curation Management

It is not always simple to develop content for marketing campaigns because it necessitates significant expense. Nonetheless, UGC allows you to effortlessly pick the greatest and most valuable material from digital channels. Also, maintaining rights to users' content and reusing it for your marketing campaigns makes content management straightforward. There are several UGC tools and systems available for managing content rights and rigorous curation. Managing content rights and curation contributes to legal stability, greater returns on investment, and the development of brand-user relationships.

9. Increases User Engagement

What are people looking for when they engage with brand campaigns? The answer is simple: engaging or fascinating content, interactive aspects, authenticity and inventiveness, trustworthiness, and value proposition are all required in marketing. All these characteristics are present in user-generated material, and when it is curated, improved, and targeted, it becomes extremely engaging and useful to consumers. As a result, including UGC in your marketing initiatives raises user engagement and increases the campaign's effect. It enhances the likelihood of your campaigns attaining their goals.

10. Boosts Marketing Metrics & Performance

UGC is the aim that marketers strive towards while developing marketing strategies. Conversions and income assure a brand's existence and success. User-generated content is the best approach for increasing conversions and income. UGC boosts user engagement, which is directly tied to conversions. Furthermore, when it comes to purchasing products or services, people prefer to trust UGC considerably more than brand promotion. As a result, UGC will add validity and credibility to your marketing message, driving consumers to conversions and increasing income.

9.6 Content is King

The adage "Content is king" has become a defining principle in the realm of digital strategy, reflecting the central role that content plays in shaping online success. This phrase has transcended mere catchphrase status and has evolved into a fundamental truth that underpins the strategies of successful digital marketers and brands. In this final section of the chapter, we will delve deep into the multifaceted meaning of why content holds such a preeminent position in the digital landscape and how it profoundly influences the art and science of web analytics.

At its core, the assertion that "content is king" underscores the pivotal role that content plays in capturing and retaining the attention of digital audiences. In an era characterized by information overload and a constant barrage of online stimuli, content serves as the gateway to engaging users meaningfully. It is the content that serves as the initial hook, drawing users into the digital ecosystem and keeping them there.

Beyond mere engagement, content is the bedrock upon which trust, and authority are built. High-quality content consistently delivers value, whether in the form of informative articles, entertaining videos, or insightful infographics. Such content fosters credibility and establishes a brand as a trusted source of information or entertainment within its niche. In an era where authenticity is prized, content is the vehicle through which brands convey their expertise and authenticity.

Search engine optimization (SEO) has also become intricately intertwined with content creation. Search engines reward websites that offer relevant, valuable, and regularly updated content. Therefore, creating content that is optimized for search engines is an integral aspect of enhancing a brand's visibility, reach, and ultimately, its return on investment.

The role of content extends far beyond transactional interactions. It is the cornerstone upon which lasting relationships are forged in the digital landscape. Brands that consistently provide valuable content tailored to the needs and interests of their audience cultivate loyalty. Such content creates a sense of community and belonging, transforming casual visitors into loyal subscribers, followers, or customers.

Furthermore, content exhibits remarkable versatility, allowing brands to adapt to the ever-changing digital environment. From blog posts and videos to podcasts and live streams, content comes in various forms. This adaptability enables brands to remain agile and relevant in the face of evolving consumer preferences and technological shifts.

Personalization and targeting are made possible through the creation and dissemination of relevant content. Effective content strategies allow brands to segment their audience and tailor messages to specific demographics, preferences, or behaviors. This personal touch enhances the user experience, fostering deeper connections and boosting conversion rates.

The viral potential of compelling content cannot be overstated. A single piece of exceptional content has the capacity to spread like wildfire across digital channels. This organic sharing by users can lead to exponential growth in brand visibility, significantly amplifying a brand's reach and influence.

Web analytics, a critical component of any digital strategy, allows for the measurement and analysis of content performance. Data-driven decision-making based on web analytics enables brands to gain valuable insights into what resonates most with their audience. This iterative process empowers organizations to fine-tune their content strategies continually, ensuring that resources are allocated effectively, and results are optimized.

Moreover, content creation and analysis provide a distinct competitive advantage in the digital arena. Brands that prioritize content as king are better equipped to outperform competitors. By staying attuned to emerging trends and market shifts, they can remain agile, adapt swiftly, and maintain a leadership position within their industry.

Ultimately, content's supremacy in digital strategy extends to its ability to deliver measurable return on investment (ROI). Through the lens of web analytics, brands can gauge the effectiveness of their content initiatives. They can identify which pieces of content are delivering the most value, pinpoint areas that require improvement, and make informed decisions about resource allocation.

In conclusion, the adage "content is king" reverberates with profound implications in the digital age. It encapsulates the multifaceted significance of content in digital strategy – from its role in engagement and trust-building to its influence on SEO, personalization, and virality. As we navigate the dynamic digital landscape, those who recognize and harness the power of content are poised to create more compelling, personalized, and effective digital experiences for their audiences. Through the lens of web analytics, brands can refine their content strategies, maintain a competitive edge, and continually enhance their digital presence, ensuring they remain relevant and influential in the ever-evolving digital realm.

Key Points:

1. Digital content is essential for web analytics, serving as the foundation for collecting, measuring, and analyzing data related to website traffic and user behavior.
2. Quality, relevance, and engagement level of digital content influence how visitors interact with a website and provide insights into user preferences and needs.
3. Digital content is a primary driver of website traffic, and effective SEO strategies rely on creating high-quality, keyword-rich content.
4. Web analytics track user interactions with content, including bounce rates, time spent on pages, click-through rates, and conversion rates, helping organizations refine their content strategies.
5. Digital content impacts key performance indicators (KPIs) like website traffic, user retention, and conversion rates, allowing data-driven decisions.
6. Content marketing involves a comprehensive strategy for attracting, engaging, and interacting with a target audience, focusing on brand positioning, owned media value proposition, business case, and strategic planning.
7. Effective content marketing resonates with the audience, balances visual and textual aspects, and aligns with SEO for better performance.
8. Content marketing guides consumers throughout their journey, addressing their issues, and supporting product or service solutions.
9. Comprehensive content marketing analysis helps understand competitiveness and industry dynamics, with internal and external examinations providing valuable insights.
10. Metrics like impressions, clicks, views, and engagement assess content marketing effectiveness.

Discussion Questions:

1. How does digital content impact user behavior and influence website performance metrics in web analytics?
2. Why is it crucial for businesses to align their content marketing strategies with the needs and values of their target audience?
3. What are the benefits of analyzing competitors' content strategies in content marketing analysis, and how can it be done ethically?
4. How can user-generated content (UGC) contribute to effective digital marketing, and what advantages does it offer over brand-generated content?
5. What role does content personalization play in enhancing user engagement, and how can brands effectively implement it?

Chapter Ten: Social Media Analytics

10.1 Introduction

In today's digital age, where **social media platforms** have become an integral part of our daily lives, organizations and businesses are continuously seeking ways to harness the vast amounts of data generated by these platforms. **Social media** has evolved from being a mere means of communication to a powerful tool for brand building, customer engagement, and market insights. To leverage the full potential of social media, it is imperative to embrace **social media analytics**. This chapter explores what social media analytics is, why it is essential, and how it integrates with web analytics to provide a comprehensive understanding of online presence and user behavior.

What are Social Media Analytics?

Social media analytics is the process of collecting, analyzing, and interpreting data from various social media platforms to gain valuable insights into user behavior, engagement, and sentiment. It involves tracking metrics, such as likes, shares, comments, click-through rates, and follower growth, to measure the effectiveness of social media marketing efforts.

Key Components of Social Media Analytics

1. **Data Collection**: Social media analytics begins with the collection of data from various social media platforms. This data can encompass a wide range of information, including user interactions, post engagement, demographics, and more. Social media management tools and platforms provide APIs that allow businesses to access and collect this data.

2. **Data Analysis**: Once the data is collected, it needs to be analyzed to extract meaningful insights. Data analysis involves the use of statistical techniques, machine learning algorithms, and data visualization tools to uncover patterns, trends, and correlations within the data.

3. **Insights Generation**: The ultimate goal of social media analytics is to generate actionable insights. These insights can include understanding which posts resonate most with the audience, identifying peak engagement times, discovering influencers within the niche, and evaluating the impact of social media campaigns.

4. **Reporting and Visualization**: Social media analytics tools often provide reporting features that allow businesses to visualize their data through charts, graphs, and dashboards. This helps in presenting insights in a clear and comprehensible manner.

5. **Sentiment Analysis**: Sentiment analysis is a crucial aspect of social media analytics. It involves determining whether social media mentions and comments are positive, negative, or neutral. This information can help businesses gauge the public perception of their brand or products.

Why is Social Media Analytics Important?

1. **Performance Measurement**: Social media analytics provides a means to measure the performance of social media campaigns and strategies. Businesses can track key performance indicators (KPIs) to assess the effectiveness of their efforts and make data-driven decisions for improvement.

2. **Audience Insights**: Understanding the demographics, interests, and behaviors of social media followers and users allows businesses to tailor their content and messaging to better resonate with their target audience.

3. **Competitive Analysis**: Social media analytics enables businesses to monitor their competitors' activities, identify their strengths and weaknesses, and discover opportunities for differentiation and growth.

4. **Crisis Management**: In the event of a crisis or negative publicity, social media analytics can help businesses monitor and address the situation promptly. Real-time insights enable swift response and damage control.

5. **ROI Calculation**: Social media analytics provides the data needed to calculate the return on investment (ROI) of social media marketing efforts. This helps businesses allocate resources effectively and justify their social media budgets.

6. **Content Strategy**: Analyzing the performance of distinct types of content (e.g., images, videos, blog posts) allows businesses to refine their content strategy, create more engaging content, and optimize posting schedules.

7. **Influencer Identification**: Social media analytics tools can help identify influencers and brand advocates within a niche.

Collaborating with influencers can extend a brand's reach and credibility.

8. **Trend Identification**: By monitoring social media conversations and trending topics, businesses can stay informed about industry trends and adapt their strategies accordingly.

Social Media Metrics

In the ever-evolving world of social media marketing, the ability to measure performance and track the impact of your efforts is paramount. Social media metrics provide the data-driven insights needed to assess the effectiveness of your social media strategies and make informed decisions. This chapter delves into what social media metrics are, lists and defines key metrics, and provides a use case example to illustrate how to select the right metric for your social media goals.

What Are Social Media Metrics?

Social media metrics are quantifiable data points that help marketers and businesses evaluate the performance and impact of their social media activities. These metrics provide insights into various aspects of social media engagement, including audience behavior, content performance, and the effectiveness of marketing campaigns.

Key Social Media Metrics and Definitions

1. **Reach**: Reach measures the total number of unique users who have seen a piece of content. It provides an indication of how far your content has traveled across social media platforms.

2. **Impressions**: Impressions represent the total number of times your content has been displayed, regardless of whether it was clicked or engaged with. It measures the potential visibility of your content.

3. **Engagement**: Engagement metrics include likes, shares, comments, and clicks on your social media posts. They reflect the level of interaction and interest generated by your content.

4. **Click-Through Rate (CTR)**: CTR measures the percentage of people who clicked on a link in your post after seeing it. It is calculated by dividing the number of clicks by the number of impressions.

5. **Conversion Rate**: Conversion rate measures the percentage of users who completed a desired action, such as making a purchase or signing up for a newsletter, after interacting with your social media content.

6. **Follower Growth**: Follower growth tracks the increase or decrease in the number of followers or subscribers on your social media profiles over a specific period.

7. **Share of Voice (SOV)**: SOV assesses your brand's presence and influence in a particular niche or industry compared to competitors. It considers the volume and sentiment of conversations mentioning your brand.

8. **Customer Lifetime Value (CLV)**: CLV estimates the total revenue a business can expect to generate from a customer over their lifetime as a paying customer. It can help gauge the long-term impact of social media efforts on customer acquisition and retention.

9. **Social Media ROI**: Social media return on investment (ROI) measures the profitability of your social media campaigns by comparing the revenue generated to the costs incurred. It helps determine the financial impact of your social media marketing.

10. **Bounce Rate**: Bounce rate calculates the percentage of visitors who leave your website after viewing only one page. It can indicate the effectiveness of your landing pages and content in keeping visitors engaged.

11. **Sentiment Analysis**: Sentiment analysis evaluates the sentiment or emotional tone of social media mentions related to your brand. It categorizes mentions as positive, negative, or neutral, providing insights into public perception.

12. **Customer Engagement Score**: This custom metric combines various engagement actions (likes, comments, shares) to create a single score that reflects the overall engagement level with your brand or content.

13. **Social Shareability**: Social shareability measures the ease with which users can share your content. It considers features like social sharing buttons and the mobile friendliness of your content.

14. **Average Session Duration**: Average session duration tracks the average amount of time users spend on your website after clicking

through from a social media platform. It indicates the level of user engagement.

15. **Customer Satisfaction (CSAT)**: CSAT measures customer satisfaction by gathering feedback through surveys or direct social media interactions. It provides insights into customer opinions and areas for improvement.
16. **Churn Rate**: Churn rate calculates the percentage of customers or followers lost over a specified period. It helps assess customer retention and identify reasons for attrition.
17. **Click-to-Conversion Time**: Click-to-conversion time measures the time it takes for a user to move from the initial interaction with your social media content to completing a conversion action, such as making a purchase.
18. **Video View Duration**: For video content, video view duration tracks the average time users spend watching your videos. It helps assess the effectiveness of video content in retaining audience attention.

Selecting the Right Metric: A Use Case Example

Let's consider a fictional e-commerce company called "TechGadgets," which specializes in selling consumer electronics and gadgets. TechGadgets has a strong presence on social media platforms like Facebook, Instagram, and Twitter. The company's marketing team is planning to launch a new product, a high-end smartphone, and wants to assess the impact of their social media marketing efforts on the product's launch.

Objective: TechGadgets aims to generate buzz around the new smartphone, drive website traffic, and ultimately increase sales. They need to select the right social media metric to measure the success of their product launch campaign.

Relevant Metrics to Consider:

1. **Reach**: To assess how many unique users were exposed to TechGadgets' product launch posts and promotional content.
2. **Engagement**: To gauge the level of interaction and interest generated by product-related posts, including likes, comments, and shares.

3. **Click-Through Rate (CTR)**: To measure the percentage of users who clicked on links in product-related posts to visit the product page on the website.

4. **Conversion Rate**: To track the percentage of users who completed a purchase of the new smartphone after clicking through from social media.

5. **Follower Growth**: To monitor the increase in followers on TechGadgets' social media profiles during the campaign.

Selecting the Right Metric: Given the objective of generating buzz, driving website traffic, and increasing sales for the new smartphone, TechGadgets should prioritize the following metrics:

1. **Reach**: This metric will help TechGadgets assess the overall awareness and visibility of their product launch campaign. A high reach indicates that their campaign is effectively reaching a broad audience.

2. **Engagement**: Engagements such as likes, comments, and shares reflect the level of interest and interaction generated by the campaign. High engagement rates indicate that users are actively engaging with the product-related content.

3. **Click-Through Rate (CTR)**: CTR is crucial for measuring the effectiveness of driving traffic from social media to the product page on the website. A high CTR suggests that the content is compelling enough to prompt users to explore further.

4. **Conversion Rate**: Ultimately, the conversion rate is the most critical metric for TechGadgets, as it directly ties to their sales objectives. A high conversion rate indicates that users not only visited the product page but also completed a purchase.

Monitoring and Iteration: Throughout the product launch campaign, TechGadgets should continuously monitor these selected metrics. If they observe that reach and engagement are high, but the conversion rate is low, they may need to optimize the product page or refine their call-to-action to improve conversions.

Social Media Action Metrics

Figure 10.1 Social Media Actions

Social media has become an integral part of our daily lives, both personally and professionally. It has evolved from a mere platform for communication to a powerful tool for businesses and individuals to connect with their audience. In the world of social media marketing, success isn't just about creating engaging content; it's about understanding how your audience interacts with that content. This is where social media action metrics come into play.

What Are Social Media Action Metrics?

Social media action metrics are quantifiable data points that provide insights into how users engage with your content and brand on social media platforms. These metrics go beyond vanity metrics like follower count or likes, diving deeper into the actual actions users take, such as sharing, commenting, clicking links, and making purchases. Some of the most common social media action metrics include:

1. Likes and Reactions:

Likes and reactions (such as "love," "wow," "angry," etc.) indicate how much your audience resonates with your content. They are a quick way to gauge initial sentiment. On platforms like Facebook and Instagram, reactions offer a more nuanced view of user sentiment.

2. Comments:

Comments reflect the level of engagement and interaction your content generates. They can provide valuable feedback and insights into your audience's thoughts and opinions. Monitoring comments allows you to engage in conversations and build relationships with your audience.

3. Shares:

Shares are a powerful indicator of your content's quality and its ability to resonate with users. When someone shares your content, it extends your reach to a wider audience and implies an endorsement. On platforms like Facebook and Twitter, retweets or shares amplify your message and help increase brand visibility.

4. Click-Through Rate (CTR):

CTR measures the percentage of people who clicked on a link in your social media post. It's crucial for tracking the effectiveness of your call-to-action (CTA) and the traffic generated from your social media posts. Platforms like LinkedIn and Twitter often use link clicks as a key metric.

5. Conversion Rate:

Conversion rate measures the percentage of users who took a desired action, such as signing up for a newsletter, making a purchase, or filling out a contact form, after interacting with your social media content. It's a fundamental metric for assessing the impact of your social media campaigns on your business goals.

6. Engagement Rate:

Engagement rate combines likes, comments, and shares to provide an overall measure of user interaction with your content. It is often expressed as a percentage of your total audience. A high engagement rate signifies a highly active and responsive audience.

7. Follower Growth Rate:

Follower growth rate measures how quickly your social media following is increasing over a specific period. It can help you assess the effectiveness of your content and outreach efforts. This metric is particularly relevant for platforms like Instagram and Twitter where follower counts play a significant role.

The Importance of Social Media Action Metrics

Understanding and analyzing social media action metrics is crucial for several reasons:

1. Performance Evaluation:

Action metrics help you evaluate the success of your social media campaigns and content strategies. By tracking likes, comments, shares, and other actions, you can see what's working and what isn't. This data-driven approach enables you to make informed decisions about your content strategy.

2. Audience Insights:

These metrics provide insights into your audience's behavior, preferences, and interests. For instance, analyzing comments can reveal the topics your audience cares about most. Understanding your audience's needs and interests allows you to tailor your content to better serve them.

3. ROI Measurement:

Social media action metrics are vital for measuring the return on investment (ROI) of your social media efforts. By tracking conversions and click-through rates, you can assess the financial impact of your campaigns. This is especially important for businesses looking to justify their social media marketing budgets.

4. Content Optimization:

Understanding which types of content generate the most engagement allows you to optimize your content strategy. You can create more of what resonates with your audience and refine your messaging. For example, if video content consistently gets higher engagement on a platform, you can focus on creating more videos.

5. Competitive Analysis:

You can benchmark your performance against competitors by analyzing their social media action metrics. This can help you identify areas where you need to improve. For instance, if a competitor's posts receive more shares and comments, you can study their content strategy for insights.

6. Goal Tracking:

Action metrics are essential for tracking progress toward your social media goals, whether it's increasing brand awareness, driving website traffic, or generating leads. Setting clear objectives and regularly monitoring metrics aligned with those objectives ensures that your efforts are on track.

How to Use Social Media Action Metrics for Analysis

Analyzing social media action metrics requires a systematic approach to extract meaningful insights. Here's a step-by-step guide on how to use these metrics effectively:

1. Set Clear Objectives:

Start by defining your social media goals. Are you aiming to increase brand awareness, drive sales, or boost engagement? Your objectives will dictate which metrics you prioritize. For instance, if your goal is brand awareness, you'll focus on metrics like reach and impressions. If it's lead generation, conversion rate and click-through rate will be your key metrics.

2. Choose Relevant Metrics:

Select metrics that align with your goals. If you want to assess brand awareness, focus on metrics like reach and impressions. For engagement, prioritize likes, shares, and comments. For lead generation, concentrate on conversion rate and CTR. Each metric serves a specific purpose, and it's essential to tailor your analysis to your objectives.

3. Establish Baselines:

Before analyzing metrics, establish baseline data for comparison. This helps you determine whether your efforts are making a positive impact. For instance, if you notice that your engagement rate has increased by 20% over the past three months, you'll know your efforts are moving in the right direction.

4. Monitor Trends Over Time:

Regularly track and monitor your chosen metrics over time. Look for trends and patterns in the data. Are there specific days, times, or types of content that consistently perform well? Identifying these patterns can help you schedule posts for maximum impact and adjust your content strategy accordingly.

5. Identify High-Performing Content:

Analyze which posts and content types generate the highest engagement and conversions. Replicate successful strategies in future campaigns. For instance, if you find that infographics receive more shares and comments on Facebook, you can create more of them to keep your audience engaged.

6. Segment Your Audience:

Segment your audience based on demographics, behavior, or other relevant criteria. Analyzing metrics for different segments can provide valuable insights for targeted content. For example, if you're running a campaign targeting different age groups, compare the engagement metrics for each group to tailor your messaging effectively.

7. Analyze Competitor Metrics:

Compare your metrics to those of your competitors. Identify gaps in performance and areas where you can outperform them. For instance, if a competitor has a higher follower growth rate, examine their content strategy and audience engagement tactics to adapt and improve your own approach.

8. Adjust Your Strategy:

Use the insights gained from metric analysis to refine your social media strategy. Experiment with different approaches and continually iterate to improve results. If you find that short, snappy video content performs well on TikTok, consider creating more of it to engage your audience effectively.

9. Test and Experiment:

Don't be afraid to test new ideas and strategies. Use A/B testing to compare the performance of different elements in your social media campaigns. For example, on Facebook, you can run A/B tests to determine whether video ads or image ads generate higher click-through rates and conversions.

10. Report and Share Insights:

Share your findings with your team or clients through regular reporting. Use data visualization tools to present your insights in a clear and understandable manner. Reporting helps stakeholders understand the impact of your social media efforts and aligns everyone around the goals and strategies that drive success.

Use Case Examples

Let's explore three use cases—one for TikTok, one for Facebook, and one for Pinterest—demonstrating how social media action metrics can be applied to different platforms.

TikTok Use Case:

Objective: Increase brand awareness among a younger audience.

Metrics to Track:

- Video views
- Likes and shares
- Follower growth rate

Analysis: For a brand targeting a younger demographic on TikTok, tracking video views is crucial. High video view counts indicate that the content is resonating with the audience. Likes and shares are also important as they signify engagement and potential virality. A high follower growth rate suggests that the brand is successfully attracting and retaining a new audience.

Action: Based on the analysis, the brand can create more content in a similar style or theme that has garnered high video views and engagement. They can also experiment with collaborations with popular TikTok creators to tap into their follower base and increase brand exposure.

Facebook Use Case:

Objective: Drive website traffic and lead generation.

Metrics to Track:

- Click-through rate (CTR)
- Conversion rate

- Link clicks
- Comments

Analysis: For a business using Facebook for lead generation, CTR is a key metric to track the effectiveness of ad campaigns. Conversion rate measures how well the audience responds to calls-to-action. Monitoring link clicks helps determine which content or offers are driving the most traffic. Additionally, comments provide insights into user inquiries and feedback.

Action: If the CTR is low, the business may need to refine ad targeting or creative elements. For improving conversion rates, A/B testing can be employed to optimize landing pages. If certain content is driving more link clicks, the business can create more similar content. Addressing comments promptly and providing helpful responses can enhance user experience and build trust.

Pinterest Use Case:

Objective: Increase e-commerce sales through product discovery.

Metrics to Track:

- Pins and repins
- Clicks to website
- Revenue generated
- Conversion rate

Analysis: For an e-commerce business using Pinterest, tracking the number of pins and repins helps gauge the popularity of products and content. Clicks to the website provide insights into the traffic generated from Pinterest. Revenue generated directly ties social media efforts to sales, and conversion rate measures the effectiveness of Pinterest traffic in converting to sales.

Action: If certain products or pins receive a high number of repins, the business can feature them more prominently. Analyzing the conversion rate can help optimize product listings or the checkout process. Additionally, monitoring revenue generated helps justify the investment in Pinterest marketing efforts and informs budget allocation.

In the world of social media marketing, success hinges on more than just likes and followers. Social media action metrics provide the depth and granularity needed to understand how users engage with your content and brand. By tracking and analyzing these metrics, you can fine-tune your strategies, optimize your content, and drive meaningful results. Social media is a dynamic landscape, and staying ahead requires a data-driven approach that harnesses the power of action metrics to make informed decisions and deliver exceptional value to your audience. Whether you're on TikTok, Facebook, Pinterest, or any other platform, the principles of using action metrics remain consistent and invaluable in achieving your social media goals.

Conclusion

Social media metrics are the compass that guides businesses and marketers in the digital landscape. By understanding and selecting the right metrics, organizations can measure their social media efforts' effectiveness, make data-driven decisions, and achieve their goals. Whether it is increasing brand awareness, driving website traffic, or boosting sales, the right metric provides valuable insights into the success of social media campaigns.

In the case of TechGadgets, selecting the right metrics—reach, engagement, CTR, and conversion rate—will allow them to track the product launch campaign's performance accurately. By prioritizing these metrics and making data-driven adjustments, they can maximize the impact of their social media marketing efforts and achieve their objectives in launching the new smartphone.

10.2 Integration with Web Analytics

Web analytics and social media analytics are two closely related disciplines that complement each other to provide a comprehensive view of online presence and user behavior. Here is how they integrate:

1. **Tracking Website Referrals**: Web analytics tools, such as Google Analytics, track the sources of website traffic. Social media analytics can identify which social media platforms are driving traffic to the website. By combining these insights, businesses can determine which social media channels are most effective in driving website visits.

2. **Conversion Tracking**: Both web analytics and social media analytics allow businesses to track conversions, such as sign-ups, purchases, or downloads. Integrating these data sources helps in attributing conversions to specific social media campaigns or channels.

3. **Customer Journey Analysis**: Social media analytics reveals the touchpoints where users engage with a brand's social media content. Web analytics can track their journey on the website, from landing pages to conversion pages. Combining these insights helps businesses understand the entire customer journey.
4. **Content Performance**: Web analytics can provide data on how users interact with specific website content. By linking this data with social media analytics, businesses can determine if social media referrals result in longer time spent on certain pages or higher engagement with specific pieces of content.
5. **Social Media ROI**: To calculate the ROI of social media efforts, businesses need to track both social media engagement metrics (e.g., likes, shares) and web metrics (e.g., sales, lead generation) in a unified manner. This integration allows for a more accurate assessment of the impact of social media on business goals.
6. **User Behavior Analysis**: Web analytics tools offer insights into user behavior on the website, such as page views, bounce rates, and exit pages. Social media analytics can provide information on how users arrived at the website and their interactions before visiting. Combining these data sets helps in understanding user behavior comprehensively.

Case Study: StyleHub

To illustrate the integration of social media analytics with web analytics, let us consider a hypothetical case study of an online fashion retailer called StyleHub.

Scenario: StyleHub is active on various social media platforms, including Instagram, Facebook, and Pinterest. They want to assess the impact of their social media efforts on website traffic, conversions, and user behavior.

Integration Strategies:

1. **Referral Tracking**: StyleHub uses web analytics tools to track website referrals from social media platforms. They identify which social media channels drive the most traffic and conversions. This information helps them allocate resources to the most effective platforms.
2. **Conversion Attribution**: By integrating data from social media analytics and web analytics, StyleHub can attribute conversions to

specific social media posts or campaigns. They discover that certain Instagram posts directly lead to purchases on their website.

3. **Customer Journey Analysis**: StyleHub analyzes the customer journey from social media to website interaction. They notice that users who come from social media channels are more likely to explore multiple pages on the website and spend longer time on product pages before making a purchase.

4. **User Segmentation**: By combining user segments from web analytics (e.g., first-time visitors, returning customers) with segments from social media analytics (e.g., Instagram followers, Facebook fans), StyleHub tailors its marketing efforts to different user groups.

5. **A/B Testing**: StyleHub conducts an A/B test on their website's homepage layout to assess its impact on conversion rates. By connecting the test results with social media analytics, they understand how different versions of the homepage resonate with social media audiences.

Benefits and Outcomes:

The integration of social media analytics and web analytics enables StyleHub to make data-driven decisions and refine its social media strategies. They discover that Instagram is a highly effective channel for driving both traffic and conversions. By focusing more resources on Instagram campaigns, they increase their ROI and improve the overall user experience on their website. Additionally, they tailor content and messaging to different user segments based on insights derived from the integration.

Conclusion

In the ever-evolving digital landscape, social media analytics has emerged as an essential component of web analytics. It provides businesses with the means to measure the impact of their social media efforts, gain insights into user behavior, and make informed decisions. By integrating social media analytics with web analytics, organizations can paint a more comprehensive picture of their online presence and user interactions.

The case study of StyleHub illustrates how businesses can benefit from this integration by tracking referrals, attributing conversions, analyzing customer journeys, assessing content performance, calculating ROI, understanding user behavior, segmenting users, and conducting A/B testing. The constructive collaboration between these two disciplines empowers organizations to optimize their social media strategies, improve website engagement, and drive business growth.

As the digital landscape continues to evolve, businesses that embrace the integration of social media analytics and web analytics will be better equipped to navigate the complexities of the online world, understand their audience, and ultimately achieve their goals in the digital age. Social media analytics is not just a tool; it is a strategic asset for modern businesses seeking to thrive in the interconnected digital ecosystem.

10.3 Social Media Sentiment Analysis

n today's digital age, social media platforms have become central to how people communicate, express opinions, and engage with brands and organizations. With millions of users posting and sharing content daily, social media is a treasure trove of information that can be harnessed for various purposes. One powerful tool for extracting insights from this wealth of data is social media sentiment analysis. In this comprehensive guide, we will delve into the concept of sentiment analysis, explore its applications, and provide a real-world example involving a well-known company.

What is Social Media Sentiment Analysis?

Social media sentiment analysis, often referred to as opinion mining, is the process of using natural language processing (NLP) and machine learning techniques to determine the emotional tone or sentiment expressed in social media posts, comments, and conversations. It involves analyzing text data to classify it as positive, negative, or neutral, thus providing valuable insights into how individuals feel about a particular topic, brand, product, or event.

The Components of Social Media Sentiment Analysis

1. **Data Collection**: Sentiment analysis begins with collecting data from social media platforms. This data can include text from tweets, Facebook posts, Instagram comments, YouTube video comments, and more. Social media APIs and web scraping tools are commonly used to gather this data.

2. **Text Preprocessing**: Before analysis can occur, the collected text data undergoes preprocessing. This step involves tasks like removing stop words, special characters, and punctuation, as well as tokenization (splitting text into words or phrases).

3. **Sentiment Classification**: The core of sentiment analysis lies in classifying the text data into predefined sentiment categories, such as positive, negative, or neutral. Machine learning algorithms, particularly supervised learning models, are employed for this task. These models are trained on labeled datasets that contain text samples with associated sentiment labels.

4. **Feature Extraction**: Feature extraction involves converting text data into numerical or vector representations that machine learning models can understand. Techniques like TF-IDF (Term Frequency-Inverse Document Frequency) and word embeddings, such as Word2Vec or GloVe, are commonly used for this purpose.

5. **Model Training**: To classify text sentiment accurately, machine learning models like Support Vector Machines (SVM), Naive Bayes, or deep learning models such as Recurrent Neural Networks (RNNs) or Transformer-based models (e.g., BERT) are trained on the preprocessed and feature-engineered data.

6. **Sentiment Analysis Results**: Once trained, the model is applied to the collected social media data to predict the sentiment of each text sample. The results are typically aggregated to provide an overall sentiment score or sentiment distribution.

7. **Visualization and Interpretation**: The final step involves visualizing the sentiment analysis results using charts or graphs and interpreting the findings. This interpretation can offer valuable insights into public perception, customer opinions, or brand sentiment.

Applications of Social Media Sentiment Analysis

Social media sentiment analysis has a wide range of applications across various industries and domains. Here are some key areas where sentiment analysis proves invaluable:

1. Brand Monitoring and Reputation Management

Companies use sentiment analysis to monitor and manage their brand's reputation on social media. By analyzing mentions and comments, they can swiftly respond to negative sentiment and address customer concerns.

Example: Consider a scenario where a major airline is facing backlash on Twitter due to a series of flight delays. Sentiment analysis helps the airline identify the negative sentiment quickly and enables them to issue a public apology and offer solutions promptly.

2. Product and Service Feedback

Businesses use sentiment analysis to gain insights into customer opinions about their products and services. By analyzing feedback on social media, they can identify areas for improvement and make data-driven decisions.

Example: A smartphone manufacturer can analyze social media comments to understand customer reactions to its latest product release. Positive sentiment can inform marketing strategies, while negative sentiment can guide product improvements.

3. Market Research and Competitive Analysis

Market researchers use sentiment analysis to gather data on market trends, consumer preferences, and competitor performance. This information aids in making informed decisions and staying ahead in the market.

Example: An automotive company can analyze social media sentiment regarding electric vehicles to gauge public interest and identify key players in the electric vehicle market.

4. Political Analysis

Political campaigns and organizations use sentiment analysis to understand public sentiment towards political candidates, parties, and policy issues. This helps in tailoring campaign strategies and messaging.

Example: During an election campaign, sentiment analysis of social media posts can provide real-time feedback on how the public perceives the candidates' speeches and policies.

5. Customer Support and Feedback

Customer support teams use sentiment analysis to prioritize and categorize incoming social media messages or tickets. This ensures that urgent issues are addressed promptly, improving customer satisfaction.

Example: A telecommunications company can use sentiment analysis to identify and prioritize social media messages from customers experiencing network outages.

6. Event and Trend Analysis

Social media sentiment analysis can help identify emerging trends, events, or viral topics. This is particularly useful for marketers looking to capitalize on trending conversations.

Example: A fashion brand can monitor social media sentiment to identify fashion trends gaining popularity among influencers and consumers.

Real-World Example: Sentiment Analysis for Tesla

Let us explore a real-world example of sentiment analysis involving Tesla, Inc., one of the world's most prominent electric vehicle and clean energy companies. Tesla has a massive following on social media, and public sentiment towards the company can have a significant impact on its stock prices and market performance.

Objective

The objective of this sentiment analysis is to gauge public sentiment towards Tesla over a specific period, focusing on discussions related to Tesla's electric vehicles (EVs) and sustainable energy products.

Data Collection

Data is collected from various social media platforms, including Twitter, Reddit, and online forums. A diverse dataset of user comments, tweets, and posts mentioning Tesla is gathered.

Text Preprocessing

The collected text data undergoes preprocessing, including removing special characters, tokenization, and stop word removal.

Sentiment Classification Model

A machine learning model, such as a deep learning model based on BERT (Bidirectional Encoder Representations from Transformers), is used for sentiment classification. This model has been pretrained on a large corpus of text data and fine-tuned for sentiment analysis.

Sentiment Analysis Results

The sentiment analysis model is applied to the collected data, resulting in sentiment scores for each text sample. The sentiment scores are categorized into positive, negative, or neutral sentiment.

Visualization and Interpretation

The sentiment analysis results are visualized through charts and graphs, showing the distribution of sentiment over time. Additionally, word cloud visualizations may be used to highlight frequently mentioned positive and negative keywords.

Findings

The sentiment analysis reveals that public sentiment towards Tesla's electric vehicles is predominantly positive, with a surge in positive sentiment during product launches and announcements. Negative sentiment is often related to concerns about vehicle reliability or stock price fluctuations. Neutral sentiment includes factual discussions and news reporting.

Actionable Insights

Based on the sentiment analysis findings, Tesla's marketing and communication teams can identify periods of peak positive sentiment and leverage them for marketing campaigns. Customer support teams can also monitor negative sentiment spikes to address customer concerns promptly.

Conclusion

Social media sentiment analysis is a powerful tool that enables businesses, organizations, and individuals to gain valuable insights into public opinion, customer sentiment, and market trends. By harnessing the capabilities of natural language processing and machine learning, sentiment analysis helps in making data-driven decisions.

Key Points:

1. Social media analytics involves collecting, analyzing, and interpreting data from social media platforms to gain insights into user behavior, engagement, and sentiment.
2. It includes data collection, analysis, insights generation, reporting, and sentiment analysis.
3. It helps measure performance, gain audience insights, analyze competitors, manage crises, calculate ROI, refine content strategy, identify influencers, and stay updated on trends.
4. Social media analytics and web analytics complement each other by tracking referrals, attributing conversions, analyzing customer journeys, assessing content performance, calculating ROI, understanding user behavior, segmenting users, and conducting A/B testing.

Discussion Questions:

1. How does social media analytics contribute to measuring the effectiveness of social media marketing efforts for businesses?
2. What are the key components of social media analytics, and how do they work together to provide valuable insights?
3. Can you provide real-world examples of how social media analytics has helped businesses make data-driven decisions and achieve their goals?
4. In what ways does the integration of social media analytics with web analytics enhance a business's understanding of its online presence and user behavior?
5. How can sentiment analysis in social media analytics assist in managing a brand's reputation and addressing public perception effectively

Chapter Eleven: Mobile Analytics – Mobile First Strategy

11.1 Introduction

Mobile devices have become an integral part of our daily lives. From shopping to socializing, information consumption to entertainment, our smartphones and tablets play a central role. This shift towards mobile-first behavior has significant implications for businesses and organizations, making mobile analytics more important than ever. In this chapter, we will explore what mobile analytics is, why it is crucial, how it fits into a comprehensive digital strategy, the importance of measuring device type (mobile vs. desktop) and delve deeper into mobile metrics.

Understanding Mobile Analytics

Mobile analytics refers to the process of collecting, measuring, and analyzing data generated by users' interactions with mobile applications or websites. It encompasses a wide range of data points, including user demographics, behavior, device information, and more. Mobile analytics provides insights into how users engage with mobile experiences, helping organizations make data-driven decisions to improve user satisfaction, drive conversions, and enhance their overall digital strategy.

Key Components of Mobile Analytics

1. **User Behavior Tracking:** Mobile analytics platforms track user actions such as app installs, app launches, page views, interactions within the app or on the website, and more. Understanding how users navigate and interact with mobile content is fundamental.
2. **Demographic and Geographical Insights:** Mobile analytics tools provide data on users' demographics, locations, languages, and devices. This information helps businesses tailor their content and marketing efforts to specific audience segments.
3. **Conversion Tracking:** Conversion events, such as making a purchase, signing up for a newsletter, or completing a form, are essential metrics in mobile analytics. They reveal the effectiveness of a mobile app or website in achieving its goals.

4. **User Retention:** Tracking user retention rates over time helps organizations understand the long-term value of their mobile app or website. It provides insights into user loyalty and the effectiveness of engagement strategies.
5. **Performance Monitoring:** Mobile analytics also includes monitoring the performance of mobile apps and websites, such as load times, error rates, and crash reports. A smooth user experience is vital for retaining users.

The Importance of Mobile Analytics

Mobile analytics plays a pivotal role in today's digital landscape for several compelling reasons:

1. Mobile-First World:

We live in a mobile-first world where mobile devices are the primary means of accessing digital content. Mobile traffic often surpasses desktop traffic, making it essential for organizations to optimize their mobile experiences. Mobile analytics helps identify areas of improvement in mobile apps and websites to meet user expectations.

2. User-Centric Insights:

Understanding user behavior and preferences is crucial for delivering personalized and relevant content. Mobile analytics provides insights into user journeys, allowing organizations to create tailored experiences that resonate with their audience.

3. Data-Driven Decision-Making:

Mobile analytics empowers organizations to make informed decisions based on data. Instead of relying on guesswork, businesses can use data to optimize marketing campaigns, improve user interfaces, and enhance overall mobile strategies.

4. Competitive Advantage:

Organizations that leverage mobile analytics gain a competitive edge. They can adapt quickly to market trends, address user pain points, and offer innovative features that keep users engaged and satisfied.

5. Maximizing ROI:

Investments in mobile app development or mobile-responsive websites represent significant financial commitments. Mobile analytics ensures that these investments are optimized for the highest possible return on investment (ROI) by identifying areas for improvement and optimization.

6. Real-Time Monitoring:

Mobile analytics often provides real-time or near-real-time data, allowing organizations to respond swiftly to issues, trends, or opportunities. This agility is crucial in a dynamic digital landscape.

Integrating Mobile Analytics into Digital Strategy

Mobile analytics should not exist in isolation; it should be an integral part of an organization's digital strategy. Here's how mobile analytics fits into and enhances a comprehensive digital strategy:

1. User-Centric Design and Content:

Mobile analytics data helps inform user-centric design decisions. Organizations can identify which features and content resonate most with their audience and tailor their mobile experiences accordingly. For example, if analytics reveal that users are abandoning a mobile app during the registration process, the organization can redesign the registration flow to make it more user-friendly.

2. Performance Optimization:

Mobile analytics provides insights into the performance of mobile apps and websites. By monitoring load times, error rates, and user feedback, organizations can optimize performance to ensure a smooth and enjoyable user experience. Slow-loading pages or frequent crashes can lead to user frustration and abandonment, so addressing these issues is crucial.

3. Personalization and Targeted Marketing:

Understanding user demographics and behaviors allows organizations to personalize content and marketing efforts. For instance, an e-commerce app might use mobile analytics to recommend products based on a user's past purchases and preferences. Targeted marketing campaigns can increase user engagement and conversion rates.

4. Conversion Rate Optimization (CRO):

Conversion tracking is a fundamental aspect of mobile analytics. By analyzing conversion data, organizations can identify bottlenecks in the user journey and implement strategies to improve conversion rates. This might involve optimizing the checkout process, refining calls to action, or offering incentives to encourage conversions.

5. Continuous Improvement:

Mobile analytics is not a one-time endeavor but an ongoing process. Organizations should use data to drive continuous improvement in their mobile experiences. Regularly analyzing user feedback, user behavior, and performance metrics helps identify areas for enhancement and innovation.

6. Data-Driven Decision-Making:

Incorporating mobile analytics into the decision-making process ensures that digital strategies are based on concrete data rather than assumptions. For example, if analytics data indicates that a significant portion of the target audience prefers using a mobile app over a website, the organization can allocate resources accordingly.

7. Agile Marketing and Development:

Mobile analytics allows organizations to be more agile in their marketing and development efforts. Real-time data insights enable rapid responses to changing user behavior or market trends. For example, if analytics show that a specific marketing campaign is underperforming, adjustments can be made quickly to improve results.

11.2 Measuring Device Type: Mobile vs. Desktop

Measuring device type—whether users access content on mobile devices or desktop computers—is essential for understanding user behavior and optimizing digital strategies. Here are key reasons why this measurement is important:

1. User Behavior Insights:

Distinguishing between mobile and desktop users provides valuable insights into how they consume content. Mobile users may prefer shorter, more visual content, while desktop users might engage with longer articles or in-depth product research. Understanding these differences allows organizations to tailor content accordingly.

2. Responsive Design Optimization:

Websites and applications should be optimized for the devices users most frequently employ. Measuring device type helps ensure responsive design and proper functionality on both mobile and desktop platforms. Responsive design improves user experience and contributes to lower bounce rates and higher engagement.

3. Ad Placement and Formats:

Advertising strategies differ for mobile and desktop users. Mobile users may prefer native ads or shorter video ads, while desktop users might engage with display ads. Measuring device type informs ad placement decisions, ensuring that ads are displayed where they will be most effective.

4. Content Delivery:

Content delivery can be tailored based on device type. For example, a news website might deliver breaking news notifications to mobile users and in-depth analysis articles to desktop users. Effective content delivery aligns with user preferences and behavior.

5. User Experience Enhancement:

Knowing the device type allows organizations to enhance user experiences. For example, mobile users might benefit from simplified navigation and prominent call-to-action buttons, while desktop users might appreciate additional features or tools.

11.3 Mobile Metrics: A Deeper Dive

Mobile metrics are specific data points and key performance indicators (KPIs) that organizations use to measure the effectiveness of their mobile strategies. Here are some important mobile metrics to consider:

1. App Downloads:

The number of times a mobile app is downloaded. This metric reflects user interest in the app.

2. App Installs:

The number of times a mobile app is installed and opened on a user's device. It measures initial engagement.

3. User Acquisition:

The channels and methods through which users discover and install the mobile app.

4. Session Duration:

The average amount of time users spend in the app during a single session. Longer sessions often indicate user engagement.

5. Retention Rate:

The percentage of users who continue to use the app over time, typically measured on a daily, weekly, or monthly basis. High retention rates indicate user loyalty.

6. In-App Purchases:

The revenue generated from purchases made within the mobile app, such as buying virtual goods or premium features.

7. Conversion Rate:

The percentage of app users who complete a desired action, such as making a purchase or signing up for a newsletter.

8. User Engagement:

Metrics such as the number of interactions within the app, screen views, and interactions with specific features or content.

9. Crash Rate:

The frequency at which the mobile app crashes or encounters errors. A low crash rate is essential for a positive user experience.

10. Mobile E-commerce Metrics:

For businesses with mobile e-commerce apps, metrics related to sales, cart abandonment rates, and average order value are crucial for measuring success.

Case Study Examples

To illustrate the practical application of mobile analytics within a digital strategy, let's explore two case studies from different industries.

Case Study 1: E-commerce Mobile App

Scenario: An e-commerce company has a mobile app and a responsive website. They want to maximize mobile app sales and improve user engagement.

Mobile Analytics Strategy:

1. **User Behavior Tracking:** The company uses mobile analytics to track user behavior within the app, identifying which products users view and add to their carts.
2. **Conversion Tracking:** Conversion events are set up to measure purchases, abandoned carts, and sign-ups for the loyalty program.
3. **User Retention:** The app tracks user retention rates and uses push notifications to re-engage users who haven't made a purchase in a while.
4. **Personalization:** Mobile analytics data is used to personalize product recommendations and marketing messages based on user preferences.

Results:

- The company identifies a drop in the conversion rate during the checkout process and optimizes the user interface, resulting in increased conversions.
- Push notifications sent to users who abandoned their carts lead to a significant boost in cart recovery and sales.
- Personalized product recommendations lead to higher user engagement and increased average order value.

Case Study 2: News Publishing Website

Scenario: A news publishing website wants to improve user engagement and increase ad revenue on its mobile site.

Mobile Analytics Strategy:

1. **User Behavior Tracking:** Mobile analytics tracks user interactions with articles, including scroll depth, time spent on pages, and social media shares.
2. **Performance Monitoring:** The organization monitors page load times and identifies pages with high bounce rates due to slow loading.
3. **Ad Performance:** Analytics is used to measure click-through rates and viewability of display ads on mobile devices.
4. **Content Optimization:** Data on user engagement with different types of content (e.g., articles, videos, infographics) informs content creation and placement strategies.

Results:

- The organization identifies that articles with longer read times and more social media shares tend to have higher engagement and implements a content strategy to produce more of these articles.
- Improvements in page load times result in reduced bounce rates and longer user sessions.
- Data-driven ad placement strategies lead to increased ad revenue, as ads are more effectively placed within high-engagement content.

11.4 The Mobile Revolution: A Retrospective

The mobile industry has experienced an astounding surge in recent years, fundamentally altering the way we live, work, and communicate. Mobile devices, encompassing smartphones and tablets, have seamlessly woven themselves into the fabric of our daily lives, orchestrating an extraordinary transformation across various industries. As we embark on this exploration, we will uncover the factors that have fueled this meteoric rise of mobile technology and peer into the horizon to discern the future perspectives on how customers will continue to wield this formidable tool.

Technological Advancements: The epicenter of the mobile growth phenomenon lies in the realm of technology. The relentless march of progress has bestowed smartphones with unrivaled power, compactness, and versatility. With speedier processors, enhanced graphics capabilities, and remarkable battery life, modern smartphones have emerged as formidable computing devices.

Connectivity: The arteries of the mobile revolution, high-speed mobile networks like 4G and 5G have expanded the realm of possibilities for mobile devices. These networks, delivering fast and dependable internet access, have unlocked avenues for seamless content streaming, online gaming, and high-quality video calls.

App Ecosystem: The rise of app ecosystems, notably the Apple App Store and Google Play Store, has been a cornerstone of the mobile transformation. These platforms have democratized access to a vast expanse of applications, empowering users to accomplish a spectrum of tasks, from productivity to entertainment.

Social Media and Communication: Mobile technology has redefined social interaction, as social media platforms like Facebook, Instagram, and Twitter have become the primary conduits of digital connection. Messaging applications such as WhatsApp and WeChat have likewise cemented their role as indispensable communication tools.

E-commerce and Mobile Payments: The convenience of mobile e-commerce platforms and the advent of secure mobile payment options have catalyzed the rise of online shopping. Mobile devices have emerged as the linchpin of modern retail, ushering in a new era of shopping convenience.

Entertainment and Streaming: Serving as portable entertainment hubs, mobile devices offer the privilege of on-the-go entertainment. Users can effortlessly stream movies, TV shows, music, and games, elevating the concept of entertainment accessibility to new heights.

IoT Integration: Mobile technology has gracefully woven itself into the tapestry of daily life through the Internet of Things (IoT). From smart homes and wearable devices to connected vehicles, mobile connectivity serves as the lifeline of seamless integration.

11.5 The Future of Mobile Technology

5G and Beyond: The advent of 5G networks heralds a new chapter in mobile connectivity. With faster download speeds and reduced latency, 5G will pave the way for immersive experiences in augmented reality (AR), virtual reality (VR), and real-time applications.

Augmented Reality (AR) and Virtual Reality (VR): AR and VR technologies will become even more enmeshed in the mobile landscape. These technologies will transcend the boundaries of gaming and education, extending their reach into remote work, tourism, and a myriad of other realms.

Artificial Intelligence (AI): Mobile devices will continue to harness the prowess of artificial intelligence (AI) to elevate user experiences. AI-driven virtual assistants, predictive analytics, and personalized content recommendations will evolve into sophisticated companions.

Mobile Health (mHealth): The healthcare landscape will increasingly lean on mobile technology for remote monitoring, telemedicine, and health tracking. Wearable devices will emerge as pivotal tools for enhancing personal health management.

Edge Computing: Leveraging the capabilities of edge computing, mobile devices will expedite data processing and diminish latency. This transformation will have profound implications for applications like autonomous vehicles and smart cities.

Sustainability: In an era of heightened environmental consciousness, mobile manufacturers will embark on sustainable endeavors. This involves the use of eco-friendly materials and the design of devices with extended lifespans.

Security and Privacy: The mounting reliance on mobile devices for sensitive tasks necessitates a continued focus on security and privacy. Biometric authentication, encryption, and fortified security measures will emerge as standard safeguards.

Mobile Payments and Banking: The realm of mobile payments will continue to burgeon, potentially phasing out physical wallets entirely. Banking and financial services will become increasingly accessible through mobile applications.

Remote Work and Education: The pandemic catalyzed the adoption of remote work and online education. Mobile devices will perpetuate these trends, bestowing users with the flexibility of remote learning and working environments.

Personalization: Mobile applications and services will intensify their efforts in personalization. AI-driven personalization will yield more immersive and tailored user experiences, amplifying user satisfaction and engagement.

The journey of mobile technology has been nothing short of extraordinary, reshaping every facet of our existence. As we venture into the future, propelled by the momentum of 5G, AI, AR, VR, and other cutting-edge technologies, the horizon of mobile possibilities remains boundless. With mobile devices poised to further integrate into our daily routines, they will continue to empower us, connect us, and enrich our lives in ways that transcend our current imagination. The mobile revolution is not static; it is a dynamic, ever-evolving force, and its future narrative is one of limitless potential.

Conclusion

Mobile analytics is an essential component of today's digital landscape. As mobile devices continue to dominate user interactions, organizations must harness the power of mobile analytics to stay competitive, provide exceptional user experiences, and drive business success. Integrating mobile analytics into a comprehensive digital strategy empowers organizations to make data-driven decisions, optimize user experiences, and continually improve their mobile offerings. In a mobile-first world, mobile analytics is not just an option—it's a necessity for organizations that want to thrive in the digital age. Understanding device type differences and focusing on mobile metrics provides further depth to the insights gained from mobile analytics, allowing organizations to tailor their strategies effectively and deliver exceptional user experiences across all platforms.

Key Points:

1. Mobile devices have become an integral part of daily life, influencing various aspects such as shopping, socializing, and entertainment.
2. The shift toward mobile-first behavior has made mobile analytics crucial for businesses and organizations.
3. Mobile analytics involves collecting, measuring, and analyzing data generated by user interactions with mobile applications and websites.
4. Key components of mobile analytics include user behavior tracking, demographic insights, conversion tracking, user retention, and performance monitoring.
5. Mobile analytics is essential in a mobile-first world, offering insights into user behavior, preferences, and demographics.
6. It enables data-driven decision-making, providing organizations with a competitive advantage and maximizing ROI.
7. Mobile analytics should be integrated into a comprehensive digital strategy, influencing user-centric design, performance optimization, personalization, and more.
8. Measuring device type (mobile vs. desktop) is crucial for tailoring content, optimizing ad placement, and enhancing user experiences.
9. Mobile metrics, such as app downloads, session duration, conversion rate, and user engagement, provide specific KPIs for evaluating mobile strategies.
10. Two case studies illustrate the practical application of mobile analytics in improving user engagement and optimizing digital strategies.

Discussion Questions:

1. How has the prevalence of mobile devices changed the way businesses and organizations approach their digital strategies?
2. What are some specific examples of how businesses can use mobile analytics to improve user experiences and drive conversions?
3. How can organizations balance the need for personalized content with user privacy concerns in the context of mobile analytics?
4. What challenges might organizations face when integrating mobile analytics into their digital strategy, and how can they overcome these challenges?
5. In what ways can organizations ensure that their mobile apps and websites are optimized for both mobile and desktop users based on device type measurements?

Chapter Twelve:
Future Perspectives of Digital Analytics

12.1 Introduction

As we stand on the brink of a new era in digital and web analytics, it is imperative to explore the transformative forces reshaping this landscape. The advent of groundbreaking technologies and evolving ethical paradigms is not just altering the tools we use but is also redefining our very approach to data analysis and utilization. This chapter aims to be a compass guiding through these changes, offering a comprehensive overview of the key trends and innovations set to dominate the future of digital and web analytics.

At the forefront of this transformation is the **Integration of Artificial Intelligence and Machine Learning**. This segment of the chapter will delve deep into how AI and ML are revolutionizing the field of digital analytics. We will explore the realms of predictive analytics, the automation of insights, and the refinement of personalization algorithms. This discussion will extend to how these technologies are adept at processing vast datasets, providing more accurate and actionable insights than ever before. This is not just a technological advancement; it is a quantum leap in how we understand and interact with vast troves of data.

Parallel to these technological advancements, the **Impact of Privacy Regulations and Data Ethics** forms a crucial pivot in our discussion. The digital world is no longer a wild west of data exploitation. Stringent laws like the GDPR and CCPA are reshaping the way we collect, store, and analyze data. This section will not only cover the legalities but will also delve into the ethical considerations that now play a pivotal role in digital analytics. The focus will be on the transition towards privacy-first strategies and the increasing importance of anonymized and aggregated data.

Understanding user behavior has always been at the core of web analytics, and this brings us to our next focus area: **Advancements in User Experience (UX) and Customer Journey Analytics**. Here, we will explore how emerging technologies are enhancing our ability to track and analyze the user journey across multiple digital touchpoints. We will discuss the evolution of tools like cross-device tracking, session replay technologies, and heatmaps, and how the integration of offline and online data is creating a more complete and nuanced view of the customer journey.

Finally, we will delve into **The Shift to Predictive and Prescriptive Analytics**. Moving beyond the traditional realms of descriptive and diagnostic analytics, this section will highlight the burgeoning trend of using analytics not just to understand what has happened or is happening, but to predict and influence what will happen next. This predictive and prescriptive approach is set to redefine the future of decision-making and strategy in the digital domain.

Each of these sections represents a key facet of the ever-changing world of digital and web analytics. As we navigate through these topics, we will not only understand the current state of affairs but also gain insights into the future directions of this dynamic field. This chapter is not just about the evolution of technologies and strategies; it is about preparing for a future where data, in all its complexity and richness, continues to drive innovation and growth in the digital landscape.

12.2 Artificial Intelligence and Machine Learning

The integration of Artificial Intelligence (AI) and Machine Learning (ML) into digital analytics signifies a profound transformation in how data is processed, interpreted, and leveraged within the digital domain. This evolution goes beyond mere technological enhancement; it represents a fundamental shift from a traditionally passive approach to analytics to a dynamic, predictive, and responsive methodology. AI and ML enable the analysis of vast and complex datasets, uncovering patterns and insights that would be beyond the reach of conventional methods.

Enhanced data processing and real-time insights stand as one of the most pivotal contributions of AI in digital analytics. ML algorithms, capable of sifting through extensive data sets, identify relevant patterns and anomalies as they unfold. This capability for real-time analysis empowers businesses to respond swiftly to emerging trends and behaviors, effectively transforming analytics from a reflective to a proactive tool.

Predictive analytics, a key feature powered by ML, has become integral to contemporary digital analytics. By dissecting historical data, these algorithms project future trends, consumer behaviors, and market shifts. This foresight is invaluable, enabling businesses to foresee and adapt to market changes, align strategies with consumer needs, and customize their approaches for maximum relevance and impact.

Personalization at scale is another arena where AI shines. Digital platforms now offer highly personalized user experiences by analyzing past behaviors, preferences, and interactions. This bespoke approach significantly enhances user engagement and satisfaction while also driving up conversion rates.

AI has also been a game-changer in customer segmentation. Utilizing ML algorithms allows for the creation of nuanced and dynamic customer segments. These segments are continuously refined as the algorithms digest more information, ensuring marketing efforts are both targeted and efficient.

Automating routine analytic tasks is an additional advantage of AI in digital analytics. Tasks like data collection, cleaning, and preliminary analysis can now be managed by ML algorithms, allowing analysts to focus on more strategic, complex tasks. This not only boosts efficiency but also minimizes the likelihood of human error.

Advancing further, AI and ML are making strides towards prescriptive analytics. This progression extends beyond forecasting future events to suggesting specific courses of action. Such analytics empower decision-makers with actionable insights, guiding them towards optimized strategies and improved outcomes.

Despite these advancements, the integration of AI and ML in digital analytics is not without its challenges. Issues such as data privacy, ethical AI usage, and potential biases in ML algorithms raise significant concerns. Businesses must navigate these complexities with caution, ensuring their AI and ML applications are ethically sound, responsible, and compliant with evolving regulations.

Looking ahead, AI and ML in digital analytics are set for substantial growth. With these technologies becoming increasingly sophisticated, we can anticipate more advanced predictive and prescriptive analytics capabilities. The fusion of AI with emerging technologies like augmented reality and IoT promises to further broaden the horizons of digital analytics.

Businesses and professionals need to invest in suitable technology and expertise to stay ahead in this AI-driven analytics landscape. Embracing AI and ML is not merely about acquiring tools but also about cultivating a workforce proficient in these technologies. Continuous learning and adaptation are essential to harness the full potential of AI and ML in digital analytics.

Use Case Example:

Consider an e-commerce company that leverages AI and ML for customer behavior analysis. By analyzing past purchase data and browsing patterns, the ML algorithm identifies a segment of customers who frequently browse high-end electronics but do not complete the purchase. Using predictive analytics, the company forecasts a high likelihood of these customers being interested in a new range of premium electronics. Based on this insight, the company tailors its marketing campaign to target this segment with personalized recommendations and exclusive offers. This strategy results in a significant increase in conversions for the high-end electronics category, illustrating the power of AI and ML in transforming data into actionable business strategies. This real-world application brings to life the potential of AI and ML in digital analytics, providing a tangible example for students to understand the impact of these technologies in a business context.

12.3 Advancements in Data Privacy & Ethics

In today's digital age, where data is the new gold, the topic of data privacy and ethics has taken center stage. With the increasing concerns about how personal information is collected, used, and shared online, the landscape of web analytics is undergoing a significant transformation. As we look ahead, it becomes evident that the future of data privacy and ethics will have a profound impact on how web analytics operates and evolves.

Evolving Regulatory Landscape:

One of the most significant drivers shaping the future of data privacy and ethics in web analytics is the evolving regulatory landscape. Governments around the world are recognizing the need to protect individuals' data and are enacting stringent regulations. The European Union's General Data Protection Regulation (GDPR) and the California Consumer Privacy Act (CCPA) are just a couple of examples of such regulations.

These laws impose strict requirements on how websites collect, store, and process user data. They grant individuals greater control over their personal information, including the right to access, correct, or delete their data. For web analytics, this means that organizations must ensure compliance with these regulations when collecting and analyzing user data. It requires a shift towards more transparent data practices and explicit consent mechanisms, impacting the way web analytics tools function.

An Emphasis on Transparency:

Transparency is a key principle in the future of data privacy and ethics. Users are becoming more conscious of how their data is used, and they expect clear and accessible information about data collection and processing. In the context of web analytics, this means organizations will need to be more transparent about the data they collect, how it is used, and who has access to it.

This emphasis on transparency will impact web analytics tools by requiring them to provide more detailed reporting on data practices. Organizations may need to implement user-friendly dashboards that allow users to see what data is being collected and for what purposes. Additionally, web analytics tools may need to incorporate features that allow users to easily opt in or out of data collection, depending on their preferences.

Data Minimization and Purpose Limitation:

Data minimization and purpose limitation are two fundamental principles of data privacy and ethics. Data minimization involves collecting only the data necessary for the intended purpose, while purpose limitation ensures that data is used only for the purpose it was collected. In the world of web analytics, this means organizations will need to rethink their data collection practices.

Web analytics tools may need to shift towards collecting only essential data and avoiding the collection of unnecessary personal information. Additionally, organizations will need to clearly define the purposes for which data is collected and ensure that it is not repurposed for other uses without explicit consent. This may require adjustments to tracking scripts and analytics configurations.

Enhanced User Consent Mechanisms:

Obtaining user consent for data collection is a critical aspect of data privacy and ethics. The future of web analytics will likely see a shift towards more robust and user-friendly consent mechanisms. This includes clear and easily understandable consent forms that explain what data is being collected and why.

Web analytics tools may need to adapt by providing organizations with the capability to customize consent forms and integrate them seamlessly into their websites. Additionally, tools may need to support granular consent options, allowing users to choose which types of data they are comfortable sharing.

User-Centric Data Ownership:

The concept of data ownership is also evolving. In the future, there may be a stronger emphasis on user-centric data ownership, where individuals have greater control over their data. This could lead to the development of data vaults or personal data stores where users can manage and control access to their data.

For web analytics, this means that organizations may need to interact with users' data vaults or personal data stores to access the data necessary for analysis. This shift in data ownership could require changes in the way web analytics tools authenticate and access user data, with a focus on respecting individual preferences and permissions.

Ethical Data Use and Algorithmic Bias:

Ethical considerations surrounding data use and algorithmic bias will continue to shape the future of web analytics. Organizations will need to ensure that the insights derived from web analytics are used ethically and do not perpetuate bias or discrimination. This includes addressing issues related to biased algorithms and discriminatory profiling.

Web analytics tools may need to incorporate features that allow organizations to assess and mitigate algorithmic bias in their data analysis. Additionally, organizations may need to establish ethical guidelines for data use and analysis to ensure that web analytics align with societal values and norms.

Accountability and Data Governance:

Accountability and data governance will be critical components of the future of data privacy and ethics in web analytics. Organizations will need to establish robust data governance frameworks that define roles, responsibilities, and processes for data handling. This includes appointing data protection officers and implementing data protection impact assessments.

Web analytics tools may need to support organizations in their data governance efforts by providing features for auditing and tracking data access and usage. Tools could also offer reporting capabilities that facilitate compliance with data protection regulations and demonstrate accountability.

Technological Advancements:

While the future of data privacy and ethics in web analytics presents challenges, technological advancements can also play a role in addressing these challenges. Innovations such as differential privacy and federated learning are emerging as ways to protect individual privacy while still enabling valuable data analysis.

Web analytics tools may need to incorporate these technologies to ensure that data privacy is maintained without compromising the quality of insights. This requires ongoing research and development efforts to stay ahead of evolving privacy concerns.

Education and Awareness:

Finally, education and awareness will play a crucial role in the future of data privacy and ethics in web analytics. Both organizations and individuals need to be informed about the importance of data privacy and ethical data practices. This includes training for data professionals and raising awareness among users about their rights and choices regarding data collection.

Web analytics tools may need to offer educational resources and guidance on best practices for data privacy and ethics. Additionally, they may need to provide organizations with the means to communicate their data practices transparently to users.

In conclusion, the future of data privacy and ethics will have a profound impact on web analytics. Organizations will need to adapt to a changing regulatory landscape, prioritize transparency and user consent, and embrace ethical data use. Web analytics tools will play a crucial role in enabling organizations to navigate these challenges while still deriving valuable insights from user data. By embracing these principles and incorporating them into their practices and tools, organizations can build trust with users and ensure a more ethical and privacy-conscious future for web analytics.

12.4 Advancements in User Experience (UX) and Customer Journey Analytics

In the fast-paced world of digital interactions, the domains of User Experience (UX) and Customer Journey Analytics are undergoing significant advancements that promise to reshape the way individuals engage with digital products and services. As technology continues to evolve, so do the expectations of users, making it imperative for organizations to stay at the forefront of UX and customer journey analytics developments. In this exploration, we delve into the evolving landscape of UX and customer journey analytics and how these advancements are poised to shape the future of digital interactions.

1. Personalization and Hyper-Personalization:

The future of UX and customer journey analytics is moving towards unprecedented levels of personalization. Organizations are leveraging data analytics and machine learning to understand individual user preferences, behaviors, and context in real-time. This enables the delivery of hyper-personalized experiences, where every interaction is tailored to the unique needs and preferences of the user.

In this context, customer journey analytics will play a critical role in tracking and optimizing the individualized paths that users take through digital touchpoints. Organizations will need advanced analytics tools to capture and interpret the vast amounts of data generated by hyper-personalized experiences, ensuring that each interaction contributes positively to the overall customer journey.

2. Immersive and Multisensory Experiences:

Advancements in technology, such as augmented reality (AR), virtual reality (VR), and mixed reality (MR), are ushering in a new era of immersive and multisensory experiences. UX designers are harnessing these technologies to create digital interactions that engage users' senses beyond just sight and sound. Haptic feedback, tactile interfaces, and spatial audio are becoming integral components of UX design.

Customer journey analytics will need to adapt to this shift by incorporating new metrics and data sources that capture the quality of immersive experiences. Analyzing user engagement within immersive environments and understanding how sensory input influences decision-making will be vital for organizations looking to optimize their customer journeys in this context.

3. Voice and Natural Language Interaction:

Voice-activated devices and natural language processing (NLP) are changing the way users interact with digital interfaces. Virtual assistants like Siri, Alexa, and Google Assistant have become ubiquitous, and users increasingly expect seamless voice interactions with technology. This trend is not limited to smart speakers but extends to smartphones, wearables, and even appliances.

In response, UX designers are focusing on creating conversational interfaces that provide intuitive and natural interactions. Customer journey analytics will need to incorporate speech and language data, allowing organizations to understand user intent and sentiment from voice interactions. This data can be used to optimize customer journeys by tailoring responses and actions to user needs.

4. Accessibility and Inclusivity:

Advancements in UX and customer journey analytics also emphasize accessibility and inclusivity. The digital landscape is becoming more inclusive by design, with organizations recognizing the importance of accommodating users with disabilities. UX designers are incorporating accessibility features, such as screen readers, voice commands, and alternative text, into their designs.

Customer journey analytics will play a crucial role in ensuring that these accessibility features are effective and that users with disabilities can navigate digital experiences seamlessly. Organizations will need to track and analyze user interactions to identify areas where accessibility improvements are needed, thus ensuring a more inclusive customer journey.

5. Real-Time Feedback and Continuous Iteration:

The future of UX and customer journey analytics will involve real-time feedback loops and continuous iteration. Organizations are adopting agile methodologies and user-centered design principles, allowing them to gather user feedback and make rapid adjustments to their digital products and services. Real-time analytics will enable organizations to monitor user behavior and sentiment as changes are implemented.

Customer journey analytics will need to provide insights into the impact of iterative changes on the overall customer journey. By tracking user reactions to adjustments in real-time, organizations can fine-tune their digital interactions to align more closely with user expectations, ultimately enhancing the customer journey.

6. Ethical Design and Transparency:

As digital interactions become increasingly integrated into users' lives, ethical design principles and transparency are gaining importance. UX designers are considering the ethical implications of their designs, including issues related to privacy, data security, and the potential for addiction. Transparency in data collection and usage is essential to building trust with users.

Customer journey analytics will need to support organizations in ensuring ethical design practices by providing visibility into data collection and usage. Organizations will be required to demonstrate transparency in how user data is processed and how it influences the customer journey. Analytics tools should facilitate compliance with ethical standards and regulations.

7. Cross-Channel Integration:

The future of UX and customer journey analytics will see a greater emphasis on cross-channel integration. Users engage with brands through multiple touchpoints, including websites, mobile apps, social media, email, and physical stores. Organizations are striving to create cohesive and seamless experiences across these channels.

Customer journey analytics will play a pivotal role in tracking user interactions across various touchpoints and identifying opportunities for integration. Understanding how users move between channels and how these interactions impact their overall journey will be crucial for optimizing the customer experience. Analytics tools must provide a unified view of the customer journey, regardless of the channel, to enable organizations to deliver consistent and coordinated experiences.

8. Emotion and Behavioral Analytics:

Emotion and behavioral analytics are gaining prominence in UX and customer journey analysis. Understanding user emotions and behavioral patterns can provide valuable insights into the effectiveness of digital interactions. Organizations are leveraging technologies like facial recognition, sentiment analysis, and biometric sensors to gauge user emotions.

Customer journey analytics will need to incorporate emotional and behavioral data to assess the impact of digital interactions on user satisfaction and loyalty. By analyzing emotional responses and behavioral cues, organizations can refine their UX designs and tailor customer journeys to elicit positive emotions and desired behaviors.

9. Data Privacy and Ethical Analytics:

The evolving landscape of data privacy and ethics extends to UX and customer journey analytics. As users become more concerned about their data privacy, organizations must prioritize ethical data practices. This includes obtaining informed consent for data collection, protecting user data, and adhering to regulatory requirements.

Customer journey analytics tools will need to support organizations in complying with data privacy regulations while still providing valuable insights. Anonymizing and securing user data, implementing robust data governance frameworks, and conducting ethical data analysis will be essential components of future analytics practices.

10. Augmented Analytics and AI-Driven Insights:

Augmented analytics and artificial intelligence (AI) are transforming the way insights are derived from data. These technologies enable automated data analysis, anomaly detection, and predictive modeling. UX designers and analysts can leverage AI-driven insights to optimize digital interactions in real-time.

Customer journey analytics will benefit from augmented analytics by providing organizations with intelligent recommendations for improving the customer journey. AI-driven insights can uncover hidden patterns and opportunities for enhancement, allowing organizations to make data-driven decisions that enhance the user experience.

In conclusion, the future of UX and customer journey analytics is characterized by personalization, immersive experiences, voice interactions, accessibility, real-time feedback, ethical design, cross-channel integration, emotion and behavioral analytics, data privacy, and augmented analytics. Organizations that embrace these advancements will be better equipped to meet the evolving expectations of users and deliver exceptional digital interactions. By leveraging advanced analytics tools and ethical practices, organizations can shape a future where digital interactions are not only engaging but also respectful of user preferences and values, ultimately fostering long-lasting relationships with customers.

12.5 Focus on Predictive and Prescriptive Analytics

The Shift to Predictive and Prescriptive Analytics: Revolutionizing Decision-Making in the Digital Age

In the ever-evolving landscape of data analytics, a notable change in thinking is underway with the rise of predictive and prescriptive analytics. While descriptive analytics have long been the cornerstone of data-driven decision-making, the advent of predictive and prescriptive analytics promises to revolutionize the way organizations extract insights and make informed choices in the digital age. This exploration delves into the transformation brought about by predictive and prescriptive analytics and how it is reshaping decision-making processes across industries.

From Historical Reporting to Future Insights

The shift from descriptive analytics to predictive analytics signifies a transition from understanding past events to forecasting future trends and outcomes. This shift empowers organizations to proactively plan and make decisions based on anticipated future events.

Enhancing Business Forecasting

Predictive analytics leverages statistical algorithms, machine learning, and data mining to identify hidden patterns and relationships within data. This capability is particularly valuable in business forecasting, where organizations can predict demand, sales trends, and customer behaviors with greater accuracy.

Initiative-taking Issue Resolution

Predictive analytics enables organizations to proactively address potential issues. For example, predictive maintenance in industries like manufacturing and aviation uses sensor data and predictive models to anticipate equipment failures, allowing for timely maintenance and cost reduction.

Prescriptive Analytics: From Insights to Action

Prescriptive analytics goes beyond prediction to recommend actions to achieve desired results. It provides actionable insights, guiding decision-makers on what steps to take to achieve their goals.

Healthcare Transformation

In healthcare, predictive, and prescriptive analytics are revolutionizing patient care. Predictive analytics can identify patients at risk of certain medical conditions, allowing for early interventions. Prescriptive analytics suggests personalized treatment plans and interventions based on patient data.

Personalized Marketing

Predictive analytics powers personalized marketing campaigns by analyzing customer data to predict individual preferences and behaviors. Prescriptive analytics guides marketers on the most effective channels, timing, and content for each customer.

Financial Services Optimization

The financial services industry uses predictive analytics for credit risk assessment, fraud detection, and investment portfolio optimization. Prescriptive analytics provides personalized investment strategies for clients.

Supply Chain Optimization

Predictive and prescriptive analytics optimize supply chain operations by forecasting demand, optimizing inventory, and suggesting efficient coordination routes and order quantities.

Energy and Sustainability

In the energy sector, predictive analytics optimize energy generation and consumption. Utilities can predict peak demand times and adjust energy generation accordingly. Prescriptive analytics recommends energy-efficient practices and investments, promoting sustainability.

Ethical Considerations

As organizations embrace predictive and prescriptive analytics, ethical considerations become paramount. Ensuring data privacy, addressing bias, ensuring transparency, and being accountable for decisions are critical ethical considerations.

Data-Driven Culture

To leverage predictive and prescriptive analytics, organizations must foster a data-driven culture. This involves promoting data literacy and encouraging decision-makers to embrace data-driven insights.

Regulatory Compliance

The adoption of predictive and prescriptive analytics brings regulatory challenges. Organizations must ensure compliance with data protection laws, industry regulations, and ethical guidelines.

Integration of Human Expertise

Human expertise remains invaluable. Decision-makers should view analytics as tools that augment their judgment and expertise. Combining data-driven insights with human knowledge leads to more robust decisions.

Continuous Learning and Adaptation

The field of predictive and prescriptive analytics is constantly evolving. Organizations must foster a culture of continuous learning and adaptation to stay competitive.

A Holistic Approach

Successful implementation of predictive and prescriptive analytics requires a comprehensive approach encompassing people, processes, and technology. Organizations must invest in infrastructure, build analytical capabilities, and empower employees to use data-driven insights effectively.

12.6 Final Thoughts

In closing this exploration of the future of digital and web analytics, it becomes evident that this field is poised for remarkable evolution and transformation. The rapidly changing landscape of technology, data privacy, user experience, and predictive analytics is reshaping the way organizations harness data for insights and decision-making.

As we contemplate the future, it is crucial to recognize that the world of digital and web analytics is not static; it is in a perpetual state of flux. The very tools and techniques that we employ today may be obsolete in the coming years. Thus, to thrive in this dynamic landscape, students and practitioners of web analytics must cultivate a mindset of continuous learning and adaptability.

Data privacy and ethics are destined to play increasingly central roles. As awareness grows around the importance of safeguarding user data and making ethical data-driven decisions, organizations must navigate these waters with care and responsibility. Embracing ethical principles will not only align with societal values but also foster trust among users and stakeholders.

Advancements in user experience and customer journey analytics promise to deliver more personalized and satisfying digital interactions. This shift underscores the significance of delivering seamless and tailored experiences across every touchpoint, from websites and apps to social media and beyond. Organizations that prioritize user-centricity will thrive in this new era.

The transition to predictive and prescriptive analytics marks a monumental shift from hindsight to foresight. Businesses that harness the power of predictive analytics will be better equipped to anticipate trends, mitigate risks, and seize opportunities. Prescriptive analytics will not only provide insights but also guide organizations on the most effective actions to achieve desired outcomes.

In this era of rapid change, it is essential to acknowledge the ethical considerations, data-driven culture, and regulatory compliance that come hand in hand with the adoption of advanced analytics. Balancing technological capabilities with ethical principles will be a defining challenge.

In this journey into the future of digital and web analytics, one constant remains: the importance of human expertise. Technology may enable us to process vast amounts of data and generate insights, but human judgment, creativity, and ethics will continue to play pivotal roles. The constructive interaction between data-driven insights and human wisdom will be the hallmark of successful organizations.

As students of web analytics embark on their journeys into this ever-evolving landscape, they should carry with them a sense of curiosity, adaptability, and responsibility. The digital world is theirs to shape and navigate, and the possibilities are boundless. Embracing the future of digital and web analytics means not only understanding its potential but also defining its ethical boundaries and ensuring that data serves humanity's best interests.

In this ever-connected world, where every click, scroll, and interaction leaves a digital trace, the role of digital and web analytics will only become more prominent. The power to understand, predict, and prescribe will rest in the hands of those who seek to harness the data for positive change, innovation, and informed decision-making.

The future of digital and web analytics is an open book, waiting for the next generation of analysts, data scientists, and digital pioneers to write its chapters. As they embark on this journey, they should embrace the opportunities, tackle the challenges, and always strive to use data to make the digital world a better place for all.

Key Points:

1. Integration of AI and ML into digital analytics represents a significant transformation in data processing and interpretation.
2. AI and ML enable real-time analysis, allowing businesses to respond proactively to emerging trends and behaviors.
3. Predictive analytics powered by ML helps forecast future trends and align strategies with consumer needs.
4. Personalization at scale enhances user engagement and satisfaction through tailored user experiences.
5. AI-driven customer segmentation refines marketing efforts and improves efficiency.
6. Automation of routine analytic tasks with ML increases efficiency and reduces human error.
7. AI and ML are advancing toward prescriptive analytics, suggesting specific courses of action for decision-makers.
8. Ethical concerns, data privacy, and bias in ML algorithms pose challenges in AI integration.
9. The future of digital analytics includes more advanced predictive and prescriptive capabilities, as well as integration with emerging technologies like AR and IoT.
10. Organizations need to invest in technology and expertise to leverage the full potential of AI and ML in digital analytics.

Discussion Questions:

1. How does the integration of AI and ML transform digital analytics from a passive to a proactive tool? Can you provide examples?
2. What are the ethical considerations and potential biases associated with AI and ML in digital analytics, and how can businesses address them?
3. How can businesses effectively use predictive analytics to anticipate market changes and align strategies with consumer needs? Can you provide a real-world example?
4. In what ways does personalization at scale impact user engagement and conversion rates on digital platforms?
5. How does AI-driven customer segmentation improve the efficiency of marketing efforts, and what are the key benefits for businesses?

References

Adviso. (2009, June 07). *Google Adwords: What kind of auction is it?* Adviso. https://www.adviso.ca/blog/tech/google-adwords-what-kind-of-auction-is-it/

Adjust. (n.d.). *Device ID*. In *The Adjust mobile measurement glossary*. https://www.adjust.com/glossary/device-id/

Amazon Web Services. (n.d.). *AWS SaaS factory program*. Amazon. https://aws.amazon.com/en/partners/saas-factory/

Angel, G. (2015). *Measuring the digital world: Using digital analytics to drive better experiences*. Pearson.

Booth, D., & Jansen, B. J. (2009). *A review of methodologies for analyzing websites*. In B. J. Jansen, A. Spink, & I. Taksa (Eds.), *The handbook of research on web log analysis* (pp. 143—164). Information Science Reference. https://doi.org/10.4018/978-1-59904-974-8

Brevada, A. (2020, April 20). *Share of voice: What it is, why it matters & how to measure it. SearchEngineJournal*. https://www.searchenginejournal.com/share-of-voice/359752/

Brooks, M. (2019, February 27). *GDPR implications for data science. Medium*. https://medium.com/slalom-technology/gdpr-implications-for-data-science-342229c62aea

Bump, P. (2021, March 3). *The death of the third-party cookie: What marketers need to know about Google's looming privacy pivots. Hubspot*. https://blog.hubspot.com/marketing/third-party-cookie-phase-out

Chaffey, D. (2020, September 3). *Search engine marketing statistics 2020. Smart Insights*. https://www.smartinsights.com/search-engine-marketing/search-engine-statistics/

Craig, W. (n.d.). *Unleashing the power of website analytics. WebFX*. https://www.webfx.com/blog/web-design/unleashing-the-power-of-website-analytics/

Davey, N. (2016, July 14). *The five steps to an omnichannel strategy. MyCustomer*. https://www.mycustomer.com/service/channels/the-five-steps-to-an-omnichannel-strategy#:~:text=Objectives%20that%20are%20appropriate%20to,by%20ensuring%20that%20there%20is

Dwivedi, Y. K., Ismagilova, E., Hughes, D. L., Carlson, J., Filieri, R., Jacobson, J., Jain, V., Karjaluoto, H., Kefi, H., Krishen, A. S., Kumar, V., Rahman, M. M., Raman, R., Rauschnabel, P. A., Rowley, J., Salo, J., Tran, G. A., & Wang, Y. (2021). *Setting the future of digital and social media research: Perspectives and research propositions. International Journal of Information Management*, 59(1), 1—37. https://doi.org/10.1016/j.ijinfomgt.2020.102168

Forsey, C. (2019). *The ultimate list of email marketing stats for 2020. HubSpot.* https://blog.hubspot.com/marketing/email-marketing-stats

Graylog. (2020, May 15). *Server log files in a nutshell.* https://www.graylog.org/post/server-log-files-in-a-nutshell

Google. (n.d.). *Google Chrome*. www.google.com/int/en_us/chrome

Google Ads. (n.d.). *How does Quality Score work? How do you improve your score? Google.* https://ads.google.com/intl/en_sg/home/resources/improve-quality-score/

Hemann, C., & Burbary, K. (2018). *Digital marketing analytics* (2nd ed.). Pearson.

Hilier, W. (2021, March 25). *What does a data analyst actually do? CareerFoundry*. https://careerfoundry.com/en/blog/data-analytics/what-does-a-data-analyst-do/

Jennings, A. (2019, February 28). *Your email marketing metrics are wrong (and how to fix them). LinkedIn.* https://www.linkedin.com/pulse/your-email-marketing-metrics-wrong-how-fix-them-alexander-jennings

Kinsey, S. (2021, February 23). *The complete guide to KPI dashboards. SimpleKPI.* https://www.simplekpi.com/Blog/KPI-Dashboards-a-comprehensive-guide

Koinig, T. (2019). *Tracking user behavior through web analytics: An implementation on the Catrobat sharing platform* [Master's thesis, Graz University of Technology]. *TU Graz DIGITAL Library.* https://diglib.tugraz.at/download.php?id=5f9018fadbb68&location=browse

Kurzweg, J. (2021, April 1). *The ultimate guide to mobile app KPIs in 2021. Bluespace.* https://uxcam.com/blog/top-50-mobile-app-kpis/?cv=1

Law, R. (2017, January 16). *The comprehensive guide to SaaS customer success metrics. Medium.* https://medium.com/the-saas-growth-blog/the-comprehensive-guide-to-saas-customer-success-metrics-1ab5fa876095

Loiselle, M. (n.d.). *3 important statistics that show how reviews influence consumers. Dixa.* https://www.dixa.com/blog/3-important-statistics-that-show-how-reviews-influence-consumers/

Lovell, O. (2018). *Artificial intelligence in marketing. finkBRAVE.* https://finkbrave.wordpress.com/2018/10/17/artificial-intelligence-in-marketing/

Madhavan, A. (2019). *Correlation vs causation: Understand the difference for your product. Amplitude.* https://amplitude.com/blog/causation-correlation

Maropost. (n.d.) *10 essential email marketing KPIs and metrics.* https://www.maropost.com/10-essential-email-marketing-metrics-and-kpis/

Mozilla. (n.d.-b.) *Using HTTP cookies. MDN Web Docs.* https://developer.mozilla.org/en-US/docs/Web/HTTP/Cookies

Net Age. (2012, July 10). *10 examples of KPIs for your search engine marketing strategy*. https://www.netage.co.za/articles/10-examples-of-kpis-for-your-search-engine-marketing-strategy

Niraula, S. R. (2019). *A review of research process, data collection, and analysis. Insights in Biology and Medicine*, 3(1), 1—6. http://dx.doi.org/10.29328/journal.ibm.1001014

Optimizely. (n.d.). *Web analytics*. In *Optipedia*. https://www.optimizely.com/optimization-glossary/web-analytics/?cv=1

Paquette, J. (2020, June 25). *Towards a World Wide Web of data. Towards Data Science.* https://towardsdatascience.com/towards-a-world-wide-web-of-data-27d5b483074f

Peterson, A. (2021, May 5). *10 marketing dashboards for visualizing performance. TechnologyAdvice.* https://technologyadvice.com/blog/marketing/marketing-dashboard/

Peterson, E. T. (2004) *Web analytics demystified: A marketer's guide to understanding how your web site affects your business. Celilo Group Media.*

Petrova, A. (2020). *The ultimate guide to content marketing strategy in 2021. Semrush.* https://www.semrush.com/blog/content-marketing-strategy-guide/

Phillips, J. (2016). *Ecommerce analytics: Analyze and improve the impact of your digital strategy. Pearson.*

Pickell, D. (2018, November 16). *Structured vs unstructured data—What's the difference? G2*. https://www.g2.com/articles/structured-vs-unstructured-data#unstructured-data

Pickell, D. (2021, May 14). *Qualitative vs quantitative data—What's the difference? G2*. https://www.g2.com/articles/qualitative-vs-quantitative-data

Price, R. (2020, May 19). *Facebook is adding Shops to let businesses sell products through the social network. Insider*. https://www.businessinsider.com/facebook-launches-shops-ecommerce-feature-businesses-2020-5

Rackspace. (n.d.). *What is SaaS?* https://www.rackspace.com/library/what-is-saas

Reeb, B. (2019, March 21). *Data governance roles: Steward, owner, and custodian. iData*. https://blog.idatainc.com/data-governance-roles

Regulation (EU) 2016/679 of the European Parliament and of the Council of 27 April 2016 on the protection of natural persons with regard to the processing of personal data and on the free movement of such data, and repealing Directive 95/46/EC (General Data Protection Regulation) [GDPR], Apr. 26, 2016, OJ L 119, 1—88. https://gdpr.eu/

SAS Institute. (n.d.). *Big data: What it is and why it matters*. https://www.sas.com/en_us/insights/big-data/what-is-big-data.html

Shah, D. (2013, March 29). *Measuring what matters: How to pick a good metric. OnStartups*. https://www.onstartups.com/tabid/3339/bid/96738/Measuring-What-Matters-How-To-Pick-A-Good-Metric.aspx

Sheffield, J. P. (2020). *Search engine optimization and business communication instruction: Interviews with experts. Business & Professional Communication Quarterly*, 83(2), 153—183. https://doi.org/10.1177/2329490619890335

Sickler, J. (2019, June 10). *How to identify long-tail keywords (and use them). Terakeet*. https://terakeet.com/blog/long-tail-keywords/

Singh, J., Nambisan, S., Bridge, G. R., & Kai-Uwe Brock, J. (2020). *One-voice strategy for customer engagement. Journal of Service Research*, 24(1), 42—65. https://doi.org/10.1177/1094670520910267

Smart Insights. (2021, April 27). *Define effective digital marketing KPIs to achieve your goals*. https://www.smartinsights.com/goal-setting-evaluation/goals-kpis/choosing-effective-digital-marketing-kpis/

SMStudy. (2017, April 14). *Heading a SEM campaign? These are a few key metrics*. https://www.smstudy.com/article/heading-a-sem-campaign-these-are-a-few-key-metric

Sponder, M., & Gohar, K. (2018). *Digital analytics for marketing. Routledge.*

Stirista. (2020, November 19). *The ultimate guide to the customer journey: Definition, stages, and mapping, and an example.* https://www.stirista.com/ultimate-guide-customer-journey-definition-stages-mapping-example

Tendenci. (n.d.). *Meaning of hits, visits, page views, and traffic sources—Web analytics definitions*. https://www.tendenci.com/help-files/meaning-of-hits-visits-page-views-and-traffic-sources-web-analytics-definitions/

Traphagen, M. (2019, January 25). *12 social media engagement KPIs that matter. SearchEngineJournal.* https://www.searchenginejournal.com/content-marketing-kpis/social-media-engagement/

US Data Corporation. (n.d.). *Target marketing vs. mass market.* https://www.usdatacorporation.com/blog/targeted-marketing-vs-mass-marketing/

Vendivel, M. (2014). *Virtual rebel website: A strategy to increase user engagement through bounce rate analysis* [Master's thesis, University of Nevada]. *UNLV Theses, Dissertations, Professional Papers, and Capstones*. http://dx.doi.org/10.34917/5836173

Ward, S. (2020, June 29). *What is email marketing? The Balance Small Business.* https://www.thebalancesmb.com/email-marketing-2948346

Weiss, E. (2020, August 27). *Data privacy rules are changing. How can marketers keep up? Harvard Business Review.* https://hbr.org/2020/08/data-privacy-rules-are-changing-how-can-marketers-keep-up

Wilkes, A. (n.d.). *PPC marketing funnel: Four stages to customer acquisition. Equation*. https://www.equationdigital.co.uk/articles/ppc-marketing-funnel-four-stages-to-customer-acquisition

www.ingramcontent.com/pod-product-compliance
Lightning Source LLC
LaVergne TN
LVHW060035210926
848481LV00013B/3866